DECODING THE SOFTWARE INDUSTRY

SANJAY GUPTA

INDIA • SINGAPORE • MALAYSIA

ISBN 979-8-89133-891-3

To

My mother, the Late Smt.Sundra Gupta (Guiding Angel),
my mentor, Parteek Bhatia (Source of Inspiration),
my supportive wife, Mrs.Annie Gupta &
loving sister Babli, sons Rishabh and Anay Gupta

Table of Contents

Preface

The main goal of this textbook is to provide a comprehensive and insightful exploration of the various departments within the software industry. It is designed for a broader audience, including students, professionals, and anyone interested in gaining a deeper understanding of the software industry. By examining the intricacies of each department, readers will gain valuable insights into the collaborative dynamics that drive successful software development projects.

By the end of the book, readers will have a comprehensive understanding of the different departments in the software industry, their key functions, internal aspects, best practices, certifications offered, and how they collaborate to create and deliver software products.

For any feedback or thoughts, feel free to reach out at **sanjay@leadsystems.in**

Sanjay Gupta
M.Tech (IT)

About Author

Sanjay Gupta is an experienced IT professional with a profound background in Information Technology, Learning and Development, Support, Sales, and CRM spanning over a decade and a half. Sanjay Gupta's experience working in different departments of multinational companies has given him a deep understanding of the challenges and opportunities businesses face today.

This accomplished professional has honed his expertise in the dynamic world of Multinational Corporations like Adobe, HCL Technologies, and NIIT Ltd. He is a Co-founder and Chief Strategist of LEAD Systems, helping companies redefine processes.

He has traveled extensively to the US, the UK, China, Brazil, Japan, Singapore, and Dubai for various project deliveries. His journey is a testament to the relentless pursuit of excellence and a dedication to refining processes.

Beyond IT, this luminary has embarked on a new chapter as a first-time author. In the forthcoming pages, you will embark on a journey through the insights and wisdom garnered from a career graced by the rigors of the IT industry. Prepare to be captivated by a narrative woven by a seasoned strategist, a dedicated educator, a process-oriented entrepreneur, and a sportsperson at heart.

Foreword

I am immensely proud to introduce Sanjay Gupta's exceptional work, "Decoding the Software Industry." This comprehensive guide offers invaluable insights into the intricacies of the software industry. It serves as a vital resource for students and professionals. It is also an essential tool for those wishing to set up their startup in the software field. Sanjay's dedication and expertise shine throughout, making this book a must-read for anyone aspiring to excel in this dynamic field. Congratulations, Sanjay, on your remarkable contribution to the industry.

Professor Parteek Bhatia
Visiting Professor- Whitman College, Walla Walla, Washington State, USA
Thapar Engineering College, Punjab, India

"Decoding the Software Industry" provides critical and precise insights into the composition of software companies. It offers valuable information on the myriad roles and responsibilities required to produce software assets. The dedicated section on Cybersecurity is an essential inclusion given the current threat landscape. This book is an excellent resource for outlining careers in the software industry. It was a great effort by Sanjay, who has wisely utilized his software industry experience to create this book.

Varinder Aulakh- Principal Cybersecurity Architect, Cenitex
Melbourne, Australia

The book "Decoding the Software Industry" by Sanjay Gupta is an excellent read for those who want to explore the different fields and opportunities available in the Software Industry. I congratulate the author for researching and compiling this invaluable treatise, which will benefit future generations.

Dr. Amardeep Gupta- Principal, DAV College, Amritsar
Punjab, India

"A Journey of a thousand miles begins with a single step." Similarly, a great and appreciable initiative being taken by Mr. Sanjay is commendable, and I am immensely proud and overwhelmed to introduce his exceptional work, "Decoding the Software Industry." The Software industry is the backbone of the modern world, revolutionizing how we work, communicate, and live. I recognize the profound impact of this industry on education, research, and career opportunities, shaping tomorrow's leaders and problem solvers. Again, I congratulate Sanjay on his remarkable contribution to the industry.

Dr. JP Shoor (Dir. PS-1 & Aided Schools)
DAV College Managing Committee

"Decoding the Software Industry" by Sanjay Gupta contains the knowledge that every software professional should know, even before they start their career. It helps the audience understand the differences within the Departments and how each department works in conjunction with others in a complex machinery called a software company. It is a must-read for anyone who wants to gather knowledge about the functioning and fundamentals of each department and can be very helpful for students as it can help them carve a career path in a specific direction for themselves. Sanjay has much experience working in different software firms, and he has put in his best effort and used his knowledge while writing this book. I want to congratulate Sanjay for this achievement and wish to see more books from him.

Himanshu Passi Solution Owner - Salesforce,
Danfoss A/S

Acknowledgment

Wow! What a fantastic drive this has been for me, a real roller coaster these last ten years. I am filled with immense gratitude for the journey that led to this book's creation. It represents years of dedication, learning, and the invaluable support of numerous individuals and resources.

First and foremost, I want to thank Almighty and my Mother (Late. Sundra Gupta) for blessing me with the courage and patience to accomplish my dream. I want to express my profound appreciation to my wife, Annie Gupta, for her unwavering support and encouragement through this endeavor. Her belief in me and my work has been the foundation of my journey.

I also owe an outstanding debt of gratitude to my mentor, Mr.Parteek Bhatia, Professor at the Department of Computer Science, Whiteman College, Washington State, USA. He was my professor at DAV College, Amritsar, during my undergraduate degree. His knowledge, dedication, and sincerity left a strong impression in my mind, which helped me survive and supported me in dealing with challenges later in my life. I thank all my professors at DAV College, Amritsar, especially Mr. Amardeep Gupta, Principal of DAV College, Amritsar, and my teachers at Army Public School, Amritsar, for shaping me well.

I want to thank my colleagues from Corporate and friends from the Academic community, especially Varinder Aulakh, who have generously shared their wisdom, challenged my perspectives, and guided me toward a deeper understanding of my subject matter. Your insights have played a vital role in shaping the content of this book.

I thank my loving sister Babli and sons, Rishabh and Anay Gupta, and parents-in-law, Mrs. Sneh and Mr. Subhash Sehgal, for their love and support.

Special acknowledgments are also due to my friends, Harpreet Singh, Jaswinder Singh, Raja Sethi, Gurinder Singh, and Deepak Shoor, for their unconditional trust and support, irrespective of circumstances.

Finally, to the readers who will engage with this book, your interest and curiosity serve as the ultimate validation of this effort. I genuinely hope this work proves valuable and enriching in your intellectual pursuits.

With sincere gratitude

Chapter 1

Introduction to the Software Industry

Overview

In our journey to explore the dynamic world of the software industry, we delve into a realm that has revolutionized how we live, work, and communicate. The software industry, a multi-layered domain, has evolved into a cornerstone of the global economy.

The software industry is not merely a collection of code and algorithms. It is the driving force behind the digital transformation of our world.

It encompasses developing, maintaining, and deploying software applications and systems that power everything from smartphones to complex enterprise solutions.

Economic Powerhouse

The software industry significantly contributes to the global economy. It generates trillions of dollars in revenue annually, providing millions of jobs worldwide. India, in particular, has emerged as a prominent player in software development and outsourcing, contributing substantially to its economic growth.

Innovation Hub

Innovation is at the core of the software industry. It constantly pushes the boundaries of what is possible, leading to groundbreaking technologies such as AI, Cloud Computing, ML, blockchain, and the Internet of Things (IoT). These innovations not only enhance our lives but also drive business competitiveness.

Digital Transformation

Businesses across various sectors rely on software to streamline operations, reach customers, and stay competitive. The software industry is pivotal in enabling this digital transformation, helping organizations adapt to the rapidly changing business landscape.

The software industry is a significant driver of economic growth. In the United States, the software industry accounts for about 4% of GDP. The industry is also a major source of employment, with over 4 million people working in software development and related fields.

The industry is also becoming more globalized, with software companies worldwide competing for market share. The software industry is a dynamic and exciting field. It offers opportunities for innovation and creativity and is a great place to work for those passionate about technology.

In today's digital world, the Software industry is experiencing rapid growth. It comprises several departments, each with its distinct responsibilities and contributions. A student aspiring to join the software industry must thoroughly understand these departments to navigate their career path effectively. This book aims to provide insights into the different departments within the software industry and their respective roles. The next section provides an overview of the various departments found within the software industry, highlighting their unique functions and contributions.

Chapter 2

Outline of Software Industry Departments

Overview

Human Resources Department

A Human Resources (HR) Department is a business division responsible for all aspects of employee management, from recruitment, hiring, onboarding, and wellness to compensation and benefits. HR professionals also play a role in employee relations, enablement and personal development, and compliance with employment laws.

Finance and Administration Department

A software company's Finance and Administration (FA) Department oversees the company's financial resources and administrative functions like financial planning and analysis, accounting, taxation, payroll, internal audit, and facilities management.

Legal & Compliance Department

A software company's Legal and Compliance Department ensures that the company adheres to all relevant laws and regulations. This includes laws and regulations related to privacy, data protection, intellectual property, taxation, employment, and other areas. This department typically has a team of lawyers and other professionals who work with the company's business units to identify and assess compliance risks. They also develop and implement compliance programs to mitigate these risks.

Quality Assurance Department

The Quality Assurance Department ensures that the software meets the highest standards. The aim is to deliver a seamless and error-free user experience. This department focuses on providing quality, reliability, and usability software products. QA professionals perform rigorous testing, identify bugs, and work closely with the programming team to resolve issues before software is released to end-users.

Software Development Department

This Department is the heart of the software industry and is responsible for designing, coding, and testing software applications. They employ various programming languages and methodologies to create innovative and functional solutions for businesses and individuals. It consists of teams of software engineers, programmers, and UX developers. This department utilizes programming languages, frameworks, and tools to bring ideas to the real world and create functional software solutions.

They also focus on developing user-friendly and intuitive interfaces for software applications. They conduct user research, create wireframes and prototypes, and collaborate with software developers to ensure a seamless user experience.

Project Management Department

The Project Management Department oversees software development projects from start to finish. They coordinate with different teams, set project timelines and resource allocation, and ensure the timely delivery of software solutions. Strong project management skills are crucial for successful software development. The project management department manages the planning, execution, and delivery of software projects. Project managers coordinate resources, set deadlines, and ensure effective communication among team members.

Technical Support Department

The Technical Support Department assists customers with software product issues. They troubleshoot problems, offer solutions, and ensure customer satisfaction. Effective communication and analytical skills are essential in this Department. They assist and troubleshoot end-users facing software product issues. Customer support representatives handle inquiries, resolve problems, and provide guidance to ensure customer satisfaction.

Sales and Marketing Department

The Sales and Marketing Departments promote and sell software products to businesses and individuals. They conduct market research, create marketing strategies, and engage in sales activities to drive revenue and increase market share. Account managers, Customer success managers, and Campaign managers are the key personnel of this department. They strategize and execute marketing campaigns, identify prospects, and display the software's unique selling feature to potential buyers.

Research and Development Department

The Research and Development Department focuses on innovation and technological advancements. They explore new ideas, conduct experiments, and develop new software solutions or improve existing ones. These departments are at the forefront of driving industry growth and competitiveness. These departments conduct market research, explore emerging technologies, and collaborate with other teams to develop cutting-edge software solutions.

Data Analytics Department

The Data Analytics Department analyses large data sets to derive meaningful insights and make informed business decisions. They use numerical techniques and data visualization tools to identify trends, patterns, and opportunities that can inform business decisions and improve software performance. They utilize various tools and techniques to extract valuable information from large datasets, which helps improve software performance and user experiences.

Cybersecurity Department

The Cybersecurity Department protects software applications from unapproved access, data breaches, and cyber threats. They develop robust security measures, conduct risk assessments, and implement preventive measures to ensure data integrity and user privacy.

Training and Documentation Department

The Training and Documentation Department creates user manuals,

E-learnings, infographics, and simulations to help users understand and effectively use software applications. They are vital in ensuring onboarding, user adoption, and satisfaction. They provide that comprehensive documentation is available to guide users through software functionality and features.

In conclusion, the software industry comprises different departments with specific functions and goals. As students aspiring to enter the software industry, understanding these departments is crucial for choosing the right career path and developing the necessary skills.

Each department plays a vital role in developing, deploying, and maintaining software products. By familiarizing themselves with these departments, students can comprehensively understand the software industry and make informed career choices. Let's start exploring each department in detail one by one.

Chapter 3

Human Resources (HR) Department

Overview

The Human Resources (HR) Department plays a dynamic role in managing and nurturing the workforce, ensuring the right talent is in place to drive innovation and growth. In this chapter, we will delve into the various aspects of HR management within the context of the software industry, exploring its essential functions, challenges, and strategies for success.

Key Functions of the HR Department

Talent Acquisition and Recruitment

Attracting and retaining exceptional talent is vital in a highly competitive software industry. HR recruiters are responsible for identifying skill gaps, developing job descriptions, and executing recruitment strategies. This involves leveraging various platforms, such as job portals, social media, and professional networks, to find candidates (the right fit) with the technical skills and cultural fit necessary for the organization.

Onboarding and Orientation

The Onboarding process becomes critical once talent is acquired. New hires must integrate into the company culture and quickly understand their roles. HR Department creates comprehensive onboarding programs to introduce employees to the company's values, mission, and goals.

Training and Development

Due to its dynamic nature, continuous learning is paramount in the software industry. HR department collaborates with technical teams to design training programs that enhance employees' skills and modernize them with the latest trends and technologies. This might include workshops, online courses, and conferences to foster professional growth and development.

Compensation and Benefits

C&Bs are essential aspects of the HR Department that significantly attract, retain and motivate employees. Compensation refers to employees' financial and other benefits in exchange for their time, skills, and efforts. On the other hand, benefits encompass various perks and services offered to employees beyond their regular pay.

Performance Management

In a results-driven industry, performance management is essential. HR professionals work closely with managers to set employee performance goals and expectations. Regular feedback and performance evaluations help identify strengths and areas for improvement. Additionally, HR plays a pivotal role in recognizing and rewarding outstanding contributions through performance-based incentives.

In conclusion, the Human Resource department is a foundation of success in the software industry. They contribute to software organizations' growth, innovation, and sustainability by strategically addressing talent acquisition, development, engagement, and diversity, fostering a productive and fulfilling work environment for all employees.

Challenges and Strategies for Success

The Human Resources (HR) Department faces several challenges while recruiting the best talent. Some of them are listed below.

Employee Engagement and Retention

Retaining skilled employees is a significant challenge in the software industry, given the competitive nature of the field. HR Department develops strategies to boost employee engagement, such as creating an excellent work-life balance and providing opportunities for skill advancement. These efforts contribute to reducing the attrition rate and maintaining a motivated workforce.

Managing a Diverse Workforce

The workforce is becoming increasingly diverse, and HR departments must be equipped to handle a diverse workforce. This includes understanding other employee group's different needs and expectations and creating an inclusive workplace culture.

Compliance with Labor Laws

HR Department needs to keep themselves up-to-date on labor laws and regulations and ensure that the company is compliant.

Managing Employee Relations

HR Department is responsible for managing employee relations, which can be challenging. This includes resolving conflict, mediating disputes, and handling employee complaints.

Implementing Change

HR Department is often responsible for implementing change within the organization. This can be challenging, as change can be disruptive, and employees may resist it.

Using Technology to Improve HR Processes

HR Department increasingly uses technology to improve HR tasks. This can help to efficient operations and enhance credibility.

Conflict Resolution and Employee Relations

Managing conflicts and addressing employee concerns is essential to maintaining a harmonious work environment. HR professionals serve as intermediaries in resolving disputes, ensuring that open communication is upheld and fair solutions are reached.

HR Department Hierarchy – Generalized View

The job hierarchy of an HR Department in a software company can vary depending on the size and structure of the company, but some standard job titles and responsibilities at each level include:

Entry-Level

HR Assistant

Provides administrative support such as filing, scheduling appointments, and answering phones for their executives.

HR Coordinator

Perform tasks such as onboarding new employees, processing payroll, and managing benefits.

Mid-Level

HR Specialist

Provides specialized support in recruiting, compensation, or benefits.

HR Manager

Oversees a team of HR professionals and implements policies and procedures.

Senior-Level

HR Director

Leads the department and develops and implements HR strategies.

Vice President of HR

Reports to the CHRO and is responsible for all HR matters in the company.

Chief Human Resource Officer (CHRO)

The highest-ranking HR executive in the company and is responsible for setting the vision and strategy for the Human Resource Department. This role reports to the CEO of the company.

In addition to these standard job titles, many specialized HR roles may be found in software companies, such as:

Employee Success Manager

Responsible for handling employee complaints and grievances.

Recruiting Specialist

Oversees the recruiting process and is responsible for finding and hiring qualified candidates.

Compensation and Benefits Manager

Develops and manages the company's compensation and benefits programs.

Onboarding Specialist

Develops and delivers training programs for employees.

Health and Safety Manager

Responsible for ensuring the well-being of employees in the workplace.

The job hierarchy of an HR Department in a software company can be complex, but it is essential to have a clear understanding of the different levels and responsibilities to advance your career in HR.

HR Interview Questions

1. What are your thoughts on the importance of diversity and inclusion in the workplace?
2. What are your thoughts on the future of HR in the software industry?
3. Tell me about your experience in HR for the software industry.
4. Describe a time when you had to deal with a difficult employee situation.
5. What are your salary expectations?

Chapter 4

Finance and Administration (F&A) Departments

Overview

In the rapidly evolving landscape of the software industry, adequate finance and administration practices play a pivotal role in ensuring the sustainability and growth of businesses. This department handles various critical functions contributing to the company's success. This chapter shed some light on the essential parts of the Finance and Administration Department in a software company.

Key Functions of the Finance Department

Financial Planning and Analysis

The Finance Department is responsible for developing and executing the company's financial plans, including budgeting, forecasting, and performance analysis. This involves predicting future economic trends and making informed decisions based on these projections.

Budget Management

The department oversees the creation, allocation, and management of budgets for various projects, departments, and initiatives within the software company. This helps ensure efficient resource allocation and cost control.

Cash Flow Management

Maintaining a healthy cash flow is essential for any company's smooth operation. The Finance Department monitors cash inflows and outflows, manages working capital, and ensures enough liquidity to cover expenses.

Financial Reporting

Regular financial reporting is essential for internal and external stakeholders. The department prepares financial statements like balance sheets and P&L statements.

Risk Management

Identifying and managing financial risks is another vital function. This involves assessing potential risks, developing mitigation strategies, and ensuring financial regulations and standards compliance.

Tax Planning and Compliance

The department ensures the company's adherence to tax laws and regulations. It optimizes tax strategies to minimize liabilities while staying compliant with tax requirements.

Investment Analysis

If the software company invests in various assets, the finance department evaluates investment opportunities, assesses potential returns, and helps make informed investment decisions.

Cost Analysis and Control

The department monitors and analyzes costs associated with different aspects of the business. This includes identifying cost-saving opportunities and implementing measures to control expenses.

Financial Strategy Development

Working closely with the executive team, the department contributes to developing the company's overall financial strategy, which aligns with its long-term goals and objectives.

Audit and Compliance

Ensuring financial accuracy and transparency is crucial. The department prepares for audits and ensures the company complies with accounting standards and regulations.

Mergers and Acquisitions

If the software company is involved in mergers, acquisitions, or partnerships, the Finance Department conducts due diligence, financial valuation, and negotiation.

Treasury Management

Managing the company's funds, investments, and financial assets falls under treasury management. This involves optimizing the use of available funds for growth and stability.

In the dynamic environment of a software company, the Finance Department plays an essential role in maintaining financial stability, optimizing resources, and supporting the overall growth trajectory of the organization.

Challenges and Strategies for Success

Indeed, managing the Finance Department in a software company can be a complex endeavor, given the industry's dynamic nature. There are several challenges that you might encounter, along with strategies to navigate them effectively.

Rapid Technological Changes

The Software Industry evolves quickly, and staying up-to-date with the latest financial software and tools is essential. Regular training and investments in technology are key strategies to keep the Finance Department efficient and accurate.

Revenue Recognition in SaaS Models

Software-as-a-Service (SaaS) models often involve subscription-based revenue recognition, which can be complex. Implementing robust revenue recognition policies and collaborating closely with the sales and legal teams are strategies to ensure compliance and accurate reporting.

Cost Management in R&D

Research and Development costs can be substantial in software companies. Balancing innovation with cost control requires a strategic approach. Establishing clear budget allocation guidelines and regularly assessing R&D projects' alignment with business goals is vital.

Global Operations and Currency Risks

For an International Software Company, currency fluctuations can impact financial results. Hedging strategies and maintaining a diversified portfolio of clients in different markets can mitigate currency risks.

Data Security and Privacy Compliance

Software companies often deal with sensitive customer data. Implementing stringent data security measures and complying with GDPR or CCPA (data protection regulations) is necessary. Non-compliance can lead to financial penalties.

Talent Acquisition and Retention

Finding and retaining skilled professionals who understand the fundamentals of the software industry is crucial and managed by HR teams, but HR makes an offer for the CTC to the new candidate after the approval of the finance team. They must ensure the CTC is competitive and the company doesn't lose a good resource.

Cash Flow Management

Balancing expenses and revenues can be challenging, especially if payment cycles are uneven. Establish cash flow forecasts and maintain healthy working capital levels.

Compliance with Regulatory Changes

The software industry is subject to evolving regulations, such as licensing agreements and export controls. Stay informed about legal changes and collaborate with legal experts to ensure compliance.

Finance Department Structure – Generalized View

In a Software Company's Finance Department, the job structure typically consists of various roles that contribute to managing the company's financial operations effectively. These roles ensure the company's financial stability and compliance with regulations. The job hierarchy can vary depending on the size and structure of the company. However, some standard job titles and responsibilities at different levels of the ranking include:

Key Positions

Chief Financial Officer (CFO)

The CFO is the highest-ranking finance executive in the company and reports directly to the CEO. The CFO oversees all financial matters, including budgeting, forecasting, accounting, treasury, and risk management.

Vice President of Finance (VP Finance)

The VP of Finance is responsible for supporting the CFO in overseeing all financial matters. The VP of finance may also have specific responsibility for one or more areas of finance, such as accounting, treasury, or risk management.

Finance Director

The Finance Director manages an Accountants and Financial Analysts (FA) team. They ensure the company's accurate and up-to-date financial records. They also work with other departments to develop and implement financial strategies.

Accountant

Accountants are responsible for recording and maintaining the company's financial transactions and preparing financial statements, such as balance sheets and income statements.

Financial Analyst

Financial analysts collect, analyze, and interpret financial data. They use this data to help the company make financial decisions, such as allocating resources or pricing products.

Payroll Manager

The Payroll Manager ensures that employees are paid accurately and on time. They also manage the company's payroll taxes.

Procurement Manager

The Procurement Manager oversees sourcing and acquiring goods and services for the company. They also negotiate contracts and manage supplier relationships.

The job hierarchy in the Finance Department is essential because it ensures a clear line of authority and responsibility. It also helps to ensure that financial decisions are made promptly and efficiently.

Keys Functions of the Administration Department

Facility Management

The Admin Department is responsible for managing the physical workspace, ensuring it is conducive to productivity. This includes office layout, maintenance, security, and utilities management.

Resource Procurement

Procuring necessary resources such as hardware, software, office supplies, and equipment falls under the purview of the Admin

Department. This ensures that teams have the tools to carry out their tasks effectively.

Vendor Management

Collaborating with external vendors for catering, cleaning, and maintenance services is vital. Effective vendor management ensures quality services while optimizing costs.

Travel and Logistics

Coordinating employee travel arrangements, managing transportation, and organizing company events or conferences are part of the Admin Department's responsibilities.

HR Support

While not directly responsible for HR functions, the Admin Department assists in onboarding new employees, maintaining records, and facilitating employee engagement activities.

Communication Channels

Establishing effective communication channels, both internally and externally, is crucial. This includes managing official communication platforms, maintaining contact lists, and ensuring consistent information flow.

Health and Safety

The Admin Department maintains a safe and healthy work environment. This involves implementing safety protocols, conducting drills, and adhering to compliance standards. This department managed all the safety measures in the office premises during the Covid-19 pandemic.

Document Management

Managing company documents, contracts, and records efficiently is essential. This includes archiving, retrieval, and secure storage of sensitive information.

Event Planning

Organizing company events, workshops, and seminars contributes to team-building and knowledge sharing. The Admin Department oversees the logistics and coordination of these events.

Budgeting and Expense Management

Another critical responsibility is collaborating with finance teams to manage budgets, track expenses, and ensure cost-effectiveness in various operational areas.

Liaison with Legal and Regulatory Bodies

Ensuring compliance with legal and regulatory requirements, such as licenses and permits, is essential to avoid legal issues.

Crisis Management

Being prepared for unforeseen situations and crises is crucial. The Admin Department's role might involve creating contingency plans and managing emergency response procedures. The Admin Department played a critical role and made all the arrangements for the transition from Office to the WFH (Work from Home) model during the COVID-19 pandemic breakout.

Challenges and Strategies for Success

The Admin Department is responsible for managing human resources to office management. Admins face many challenges, including:

Managing a High Volume of Work

Admins are often responsible for handling paperwork, emails, and other administrative tasks. This can be a challenge to stay organized and on top of everything.

Meeting the Needs of a Fast-Paced Environment

Software companies are often fast-paced and constantly evolving. This can make it a challenge for admins to keep up with the latest changes and ensure that they are meeting the needs of their team members.

Balancing the Needs of Different Departments

Admins often have to balance the needs of various departments within the company. Ensuring that everyone receives the necessary support can be challenging.

Despite these challenges, they work on several strategies listed below to succeed in their role.

Being Organized and Efficient

Admins need to stay organized and efficient to manage their workload. This includes using tools and techniques to help them prioritize their tasks.

Being Proactive

Admins need to be proactive in anticipating the needs of their team members and taking steps to meet those needs. This can help to avoid problems and ensure that everyone is happy.

Being Flexible

Admins need to be flexible and adaptable to keep up with the changes in their environment. This includes being willing to learn new things and take on new challenges.

By following these strategies, admins can overcome their challenges and succeed.

Administration Dept. Structure – Generalized View

The job hierarchy in the Admin Department in a software company can vary depending on the size and structure of the company. However, some standard job titles and their corresponding levels in the hierarchy might include the following:

Entry-Level

Receptionist

Receptionists are responsible for greeting guests and answering phones. They typically have some administrative experience.

Mid-Level

Senior Administrative Assistant

Senior Administrative is a highly experienced professional who supports senior managers and executives. They have a strong understanding of office procedures and can work independently and as part of a team.

EA

Executive Assistants provide administrative support to senior executives. An executive assistant's duties and responsibilities may include scheduling appointments, drafting emails, and arranging travel and accommodation.

Senior-Level

Director of Administration

The Director is responsible for the overall administrative operations of the organization. They oversee facilities management (procurement, environmental compliance, operations).

Vice President of Administration

They develop and implement strategic plans. They typically report to the CAO.

Chief Administrative Officer (CAO)

The CAO is the highest-ranking administrative position in a company. They oversee and coordinate with other functions, such as HR, Finance, and IT. The CAO typically reports to the CEO or another senior executive.

Ultimately, the job hierarchy in the Admin Department is designed to ensure that executive functions are managed effectively and efficiently.

Finance and Admin Interview Questions

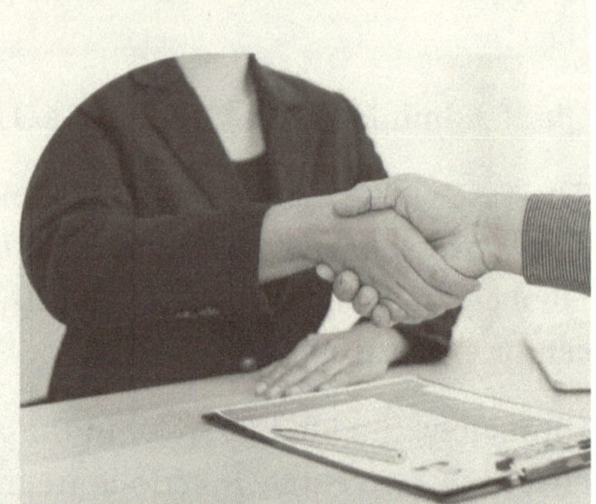

1. What is your experience with financial reporting and analysis for software companies?
2. What is your experience with budgeting and forecasting for software companies?
3. What is your experience with financial risk management for software companies?
4. What is your experience with financial systems and software?
5. How do you prioritize your work when you have multiple tasks?
6. How do you handle challenging situations with colleagues, clients, or the organization level?

Chapter 5

Legal and Compliance Department

Overview

A software company's Legal and Compliance Department refers to the processes and procedures that comply with all applicable laws, regulations, and industry standards. This includes rules and regulations related to privacy, security, intellectual property, and employment.

Key Functions of the Legal & Compliance

Ensure that a company complies with all applicable laws and regulations, including a wide range of activities, such as:

Providing Legal Advice to the Company

The team can provide legal advice to the company on a variety of matters, such as:

- The negotiation of contracts
- The development of new products or services
- The resolution of legal disputes
- The expansion of the company's operations into new markets

Overseeing Compliance with Laws and Regulations

The Legal team develops compliance programs to safeguard the company's agreement with all applicable laws and regulations. These programs can include:

- The creation of policies and procedures
- The monitoring of compliance
- The auditing of compliance
- The provision of training to employees

Investigating Potential Legal Violations

If the Legal team suspects the company has violated a law or regulation, they can investigate and take appropriate action. This may include:

- Interviewing employees
- Reviewing documents
- Conducting an internal audit
- Reporting the issue to law enforcement

Negotiating Contracts

The Legal team can negotiate contracts on behalf of the company to ensure that they are in the company's best interests. This includes:

- Negotiating the terms of the contract
- Reviewing the contract for any potential legal risks
- Confirming that the agreement complies with applicable laws and regulations

Drafting and Reviewing Legal Documents

The Legal team can draft and check a variety of legal documents, such as:

- Contracts
- Employee handbooks
- Regulatory filings
- Patent applications
- Trademark registrations

Advising on Risk Management

The Legal team can recommend that the company identify and manage legal risks. This includes:

- Identifying potential legal risks
- Developing strategies to mitigate legal risks
- Responding to legal threats that have arisen

Protecting the Company's Assets

The Legal team can help protect it by ensuring it complies with laws and regulations and preventing fraud and other illegal activities. This includes:

- Developing and implementing internal controls
- Conducting background checks on employees
- Monitoring for suspicious activity
- Investigating allegations of fraud

The Legal and Compliance team is a crucial part of any organization. By effectively carrying out its essential functions, the company can avoid fines and penalties, protect its reputation, and maintain a solid legal foundation for its business operations.

Challenges and Strategies for Success

The Legal and Compliance Department faces several challenges in today's complex and ever-changing business environment. Some of the most common challenges include:

Rapidly Changing Regulations

The Legal and Compliance professionals must stay up-to-date on a constantly evolving regulatory landscape. This can be daunting, given the sheer volume of rules businesses must abide by.

Complex Legal Issues

The Legal and Compliance department often addresses data privacy, intellectual property, and employment law issues. These issues can be challenging to understand and navigate, even for experienced professionals.

Increased Scrutiny

Businesses are facing increased scrutiny from regulators and the public. The Legal and Compliance Department must proactively identify and address potential risks.

Despite these challenges, there are several strategies that the Legal and Compliance Departments use to achieve success. Some of these strategies include:

Focus on Risk Management

The Legal and Compliance Department identifies and manages risks. It is achieved by conducting regular risk assessments and developing mitigation plans.

Build Relationships with Key Stakeholders

The Legal and Compliance Department manages relationships with key stakeholders, such as executives, employees, and regulators. This guarantees that all individuals are aligned and share a cohesive comprehension of the company's goals and objectives.

Use Technology to Automate Tasks

The Legal and Compliance Department can automate document review and compliance reporting tasks. This can free up staff time to focus on more strategic work.

Invest in Training and Development

The Legal and Compliance Department invests in training and development for their staff. This ensures that employees have the necessary skills and knowledge to meet the standards.

Privacy

Software companies must comply with laws and regulations that protect the confidentiality of personal information.

Security

Software companies must safeguard their systems and data from unauthenticated access, use, disclosure, modification, or destruction. This involves implementing appropriate security controls, such as access controls, encryption, and disaster recovery plans.

Intellectual Property

Software companies must protect their rights, including copyrights, trademarks, and patents. This includes registering their intellectual property with the appropriate authorities and taking steps to enforce their rights against infringers.

Employment

Software companies must comply with laws and regulations that govern the profession, such as anti-discrimination, wage and hour, and labor laws. This includes ensuring they are paying their employees somewhat, providing them safe working conditions, and respecting their rights.

These strategies help protect businesses from legal and regulatory risks. They also help to ensure that their companies are operating correctly and ethically.

Legal & Compliance Dept. Structure –Generalized View

The job hierarchy in the Legal and Compliance Department in the software industry typically follows this order:

Chief Legal Officer (CLO)

The CLO is the highest-ranking legal official in a company and is responsible for driving and overseeing all legal affairs. They typically have a law degree and many years of experience in the legal field.

Vice President of Legal Affairs

The VP of Legal Affairs reports to the Chief Legal Officer (CLO) and oversees the day-to-day operations of the Legal department. They typically have a law degree and several years of experience in the software industry.

Legal Director

The Legal Director reports to the Vice President of Legal Affairs and oversees a specific area of legal practice, such as intellectual property law or regulatory compliance. They typically have a law degree and several years of experience in the software industry.

Senior Counsel

Senior Counsel reports to the Legal Director and is responsible for providing legal advice and counsel to business units within the company. They typically have a law degree and several years of experience in the software industry.

Associate Counsel

Associate Counsel reports to the Senior Counsel and provides legal support to business units within the company. They typically have a law degree and less experience than Senior Counsel.

Legal Assistant

Legal Assistants deliver administrative support to the Legal Department. They typically do not have a law degree.

The job roles and responsibilities may differ depending on the size and structure of the company. However, the job hierarchy typically follows this general pattern.

Here are some of the critical responsibilities of the Legal and Compliance Department in the software industry:

- Overseeing all company legal affairs, including providing legal advice and counsel to business units, negotiating contracts, and managing intellectual property.
- Ensures compliance, including anti-corruption and data privacy laws.
- Training employees on legal and compliance issues. This helps employees understand their legal responsibilities and how to comply with company policies.
- Investigating and resolving legal claims includes investigating allegations of wrongdoing and negotiating settlements.
- Representing the company in court may be necessary if the company is sued.

The Legal and Compliance Department ensures that software companies operate lawfully and ethically. By providing legal advice and counsel, ensuring compliance with laws and regulations, and training employees on legal and compliance issues, the Legal and Compliance Department helps to protect the company from legal liability and reputational damage.

Legal & Compliance Interview Questions

1. What are some key legal and compliance risks facing software companies today?
2. How would you approach developing and implementing a compliance program for a software company?
3. What experience do you have with drafting and reviewing software contracts?
4. How would you handle a situation where you discovered that a software product violated a customer's privacy rights?
5. What are your thoughts on the ethical implications of artificial intelligence?

Chapter 6

Software Development Department

Overview

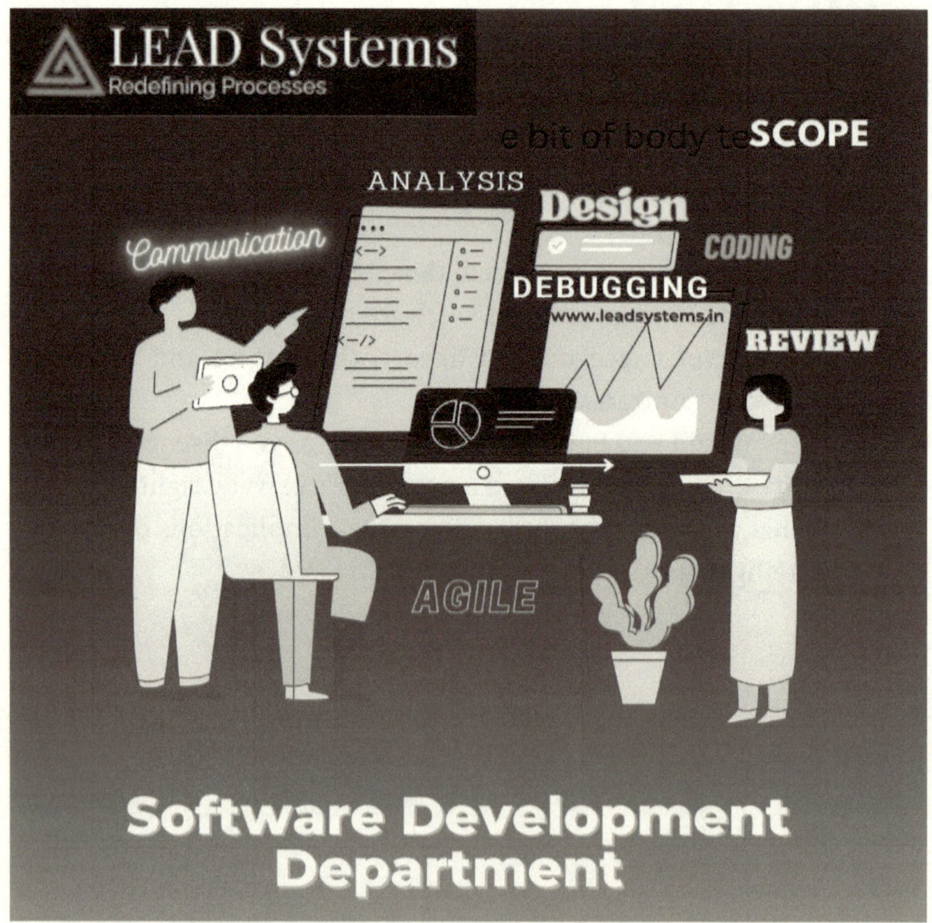

The Software Development Department is responsible for designing, coding, testing, and maintaining software applications. The primary role of these teams is to transform the requirements and specifications provided by clients or stakeholders into functional software solutions. They use their technical expertise to write code, develop algorithms, and design user interfaces that meet the end-user's expectations.

This chapter aims to provide a comprehensive view of the software development teams the backbones of any successful software project. The R&Rs (roles and responsibilities) can vary according to the size and structure of the company, the specific task being worked on, and the methodology being used.

The roles and responsibilities within a Software Development Department are critical to creating and maintaining software products. Here's a subjective breakdown of the vital functions and their corresponding duties within a Software Development Department:

Software Developer

Design, develop, test, and maintain software applications and solutions according to project requirements. Collaborate with cross-functional teams to ensure code quality, functionality, and performance.

Software Engineer

Apply engineering principles to software development processes. Design scalable architectures, analyze technical requirements, and implement robust solutions. Collaborate with stakeholders to align software projects with business goals.

Frontend Developer

Create user interfaces and interactive elements for software applications. Translate design mock-ups into functional interfaces using programming languages and frameworks. Ensure responsive design and optimal user experience.

Backend Developer

Develop and maintain server-side logic, databases, and APIs to support front-end functionality. Optimize server performance, security, and scalability while managing data storage and retrieval.

Full Stack Developer

Combines frontend and backend skills to create end-to-end solutions. Handle both client-side and server-side development, ensuring seamless communication and integration between components.

Quality Assurance (QA) Engineer

Test software applications rigorously to identify defects, inconsistencies, and performance issues. Develop and execute testing plans, conduct automated and manual tests, and ensure software meets quality standards.

DevOps Engineer

Automate deployment, testing, and monitoring processes to enhance development efficiency. Manage infrastructure, implement continuous integration/continuous deployment (CI/CD) pipelines, and ensure smooth software releases.

UI/UX Designer

Create intuitive and visually appealing user interfaces. Conduct user research, design prototypes, and collaborate with developers to implement designs that provide exceptional user experiences.

Product Manager

Define software product vision, strategy, and roadmap. Collaborate with stakeholders to gather requirements, prioritize features, and manage the development lifecycle. Ensure the final product aligns with user needs and business goals.

Project Manager

Plan, execute, and monitor software development projects. Define project scope, allocate resources, watch budget constraints, track progress, manage risks, and ensure deadlines are met.

These roles collectively form the foundation of a Software Development Department.

Key Functions of the Software Development Team

In the realm of software development, the success of any project pivots upon the effective collaboration and synchronized efforts of a dedicated team. This section delves into the essential functions of a software development team, highlighting the critical roles each member plays in the pursuit of creating innovative, high-quality software solutions.

Project Planning and Management

A robust project management and planning function is at the heart of every successful software development project. This role involves defining project scope, setting goals, allocating resources, creating timelines, and managing risks.

Requirement Analysis

The team must thoroughly analyze requirements to create software that aligns with your strategic goals. This phase involves working closely with stakeholders to understand their needs and expectations.

Development and Coding

The heart of software development lies in the hands of the developers and coders. These individuals bring the designs to life, writing code that transforms concepts into functional software. It requires meticulous attention to detail, adherence to coding standards, and constant iteration to refine and optimize the codebase.

Software Architecture and Design

The software architecture and design function involve envisioning the overarching structure of the software and designing its components. The software architecture is the blueprint, while the design is the detailed plan. Experienced professionals in this role collaborate closely with stakeholders to ensure that the software's architecture aligns with its intended purpose, scalability, and maintainability.

Quality Assurance and Testing

QA can be a separate department or can be considered within the S/W development department, depending on the size and structure of the company. I have covered QA as a different department with detailed information later in the book. In the pursuit of delivering reliable software, the quality assurance and testing function plays a pivotal role. This function systematically tests the software for bugs, errors, and vulnerabilities, ensuring its functionality meets user expectations.

User Experience (UX) and User Interface (UI) Design

The UX and UI design function creates an intuitive and visually appealing user interface. This involves understanding user behavior, designing seamless interactions, and ensuring the software is user-friendly and engaging.

Deployment and DevOps

Once the software is developed and tested, the Deployment and DevOps functions come into play. This involves automating deployment processes, managing infrastructure, and ensuring the software can be deployed reliably and efficiently.

Continuous Improvement and Innovation

Continuous improvement and innovation are crucial in the rapidly evolving software development landscape. This role involves staying updated with emerging technologies, exploring new methodologies, and seeking ways to enhance the software's performance and features.

Maintenance and Support

Even after deployment, the software development team remains involved in ongoing maintenance and support. Regular updates, bug fixes, and user support are critical to running the software smoothly.

In conclusion, the critical functions of a software development team entwine seamlessly, each contributing to the creation of exceptional software solutions.

Challenges and Strategies for Success

Creating and maintaining an organization's software falls under the responsibility of the software development department. Given the numerous factors that must be considered, it is a demanding and challenging undertaking. These factors include the software requirements, budget constraints, project timeline, and team members' proficiency. Some of the most common challenges faced by software development departments include:

Unclear Requirements

The first step in any software development project is to gather the requirements from the stakeholders. However, this can be difficult, as stakeholders often have different and conflicting ideas about what they want.

Tight Deadlines

Software development projects often have tight deadlines, leading to stress and burnout among team members.

Insufficient Resources

Software development projects often require a lot of resources, such as money, time, and people. However, organizations may not have the resources needed, leading to delays and cost overruns.

Rapid Technological Evolution

Software development can be technically challenging, as there are many different platforms and programming languages to choose from. It can be a challenge for teams not well-versed in the latest technologies.

Communication Problems

Communication problems can be a significant obstacle to success in software development. This is because software development is a collaborative effort, and it is essential for all team members to be on the same page.

Scope Creep

Uncontrolled expansion of project scope can hinder development timelines and budgets.

Some of the strategies used to overcome these challenges and succeed in software development are:

Agile Development

Agile Development is a methodology that breaks down software development into smaller, more manageable tasks. This can help to reduce the risk of delays and cost overruns. The topic is covered in detail in a later part.

Continuous Integration and Delivery (CI/CD)

It streamlines the software development process by automating the building, testing, and deployment stages. By doing so, it enhances software quality and expedites the introduction of new features to the market.

DevOps

DevOps aims to foster a collaborative culture among development, operations, and security teams, enabling them to work together more efficiently.

Training and Development

Training and Development for software developers can help improve their skills and knowledge. This can lead to better-quality software and a more productive team.

Collaboration

Effective collaboration establishes a suitable environment for sharing ideas and feedback sessions.

Project Management Tools

The team utilizes Jira, Trello, or Asana to streamline project management and collaboration.

Clear Communication Channels

Regular and clear communication between technical and non-technical teams helps to bridge the gap. This will help to ensure that all team members are on the same page and that the project is completed on time and within budget.

Robust Cybersecurity Protocols

Implement strict security measures, conduct regular audits, and stay updated on emerging threats.

Scope Management

Employ effective scope control mechanisms to prevent scope creep and maintain project focus.

Important Terminology used in this Department

1. Agile Development Methodologies

Agile Development Methodologies are software development processes emphasizing iterative development, incremental delivery, and customer collaboration. Agile methodologies are designed to adapt to changing requirements and to deliver working software more quickly than traditional waterfall methods. This topic will provide an introduction, explaining its principles and benefits for multiple departments within the software industry.

Agile methodologies provide a framework for efficient and effective project management for the software development department. Due to the iterative nature of Agile, regular feedback from stakeholders ensures that the end product meets their expectations. By breaking down the development process into more minor, manageable chunks called Sprints, development teams can verify and resolve issues early on, reducing the risk of costly rework.

Several widely adopted Agile Development Methodologies include:

Scrum

Scrum is a simplified framework designed to effectively manage complex projects. It is based on breaking down projects into smaller, more manageable pieces called Sprints. Sprints typically last two to four weeks. During each sprint, a cross-functional team completes predefined tasks from the product backlog. Daily hurdles are held to discuss progress, challenges, and plans for the day.

At the end of each sprint, a review meeting is conducted to showcase the completed work to stakeholders, and a retrospective meeting is held to analyze what went well and what could be improved in the next sprint.

Scrum promotes adaptability, continuous improvement, and collaboration among team members.

Extreme Programming (XP)

XP aims to rapidly deliver high-quality software by adopting values and practices. XP emphasizes simplicity, communication, feedback, and continuous testing.

Kanban

Kanban helps teams visualize work, limit work-in-progress (WIP), and optimize workflow. It is based on pulling work through the system rather than pushing it. This means that work items are only started when they can be completed.

Feature-Driven Development (FDD)

FDD is a software development methodology that identifies and delivers features. Features are defined as the most minor units of application that can be delivered to the customer.

Dynamic Systems Development Method (DSDM)

DSDM emphasizes flexibility and iterative development. It is based on working closely with the customer to define and deliver requirements.

The best Agile Development Methodology for a particular project will depend on the project's and the team's specific needs. However, all agile methods share the following common characteristics:

Iterative development

Agile methodologies break down projects into smaller, more manageable pieces that are developed and delivered iteratively. This allows for quick changes as the project progresses.

Incremental delivery

Agile methodologies deliver working software to the customer regularly. This allows the customer to provide feedback early and often, which helps to ensure that the final product meets their needs.

Customer collaboration

Agile methodologies emphasize close cooperation between the development and customer teams. The main objective is to guarantee that the customer's requirements are fulfilled with timely delivery and allocated budget.

If you are considering using an agile development methodology for your next project, there are a few things you should keep in mind:

Agile methods require a change in mindset

We are required to adopt the idea of continuous improvement and adaptation. This can be a challenge for teams using traditional waterfall methods.

Agile methodologies require strong communication

Agile methods rely on close collaboration between the development team and the customer.

Agile methodologies require a commitment to change

Agile methodologies are not a one-size-fits-all solution. They need a commitment to change and adaptation from everyone involved in the project.

In conclusion, Agile Development Methodologies have revolutionized the software industry by providing a flexible and collaborative approach to project management and results in enhancing productivity, improving customer satisfaction, and driving innovation in an ever-changing landscape. Its principles and benefits extend beyond the software development department to various other departments within the industry.

2. Collaboration and Communication in Software Dev.

Effective collaboration and communication are the pillars for the success of any software development project. The software industry department must collaborate seamlessly to deliver high-quality products and solutions in today's fast-paced and interconnected world. This topic covers the importance of collaboration and communication in various software industry departments and how they contribute to the overall success of software development projects.

Software Development Department

Collaboration and communication within the software development department are critical to ensure smooth coding, testing, and debugging activities. Developers must coordinate their efforts, share knowledge, and work together to solve complex problems. Communication tools like project management software, version control systems, and code review platforms facilitate team members' collaboration. Regular team meetings, stand-ups, and code reviews foster effective communication and ensure everyone is on the same page.

Quality Assurance Department

Collaboration and communication are essential for the quality assurance department to understand project requirements, create test plans, and report bugs. Clear communication between quality assurance analysts and developers helps identify and resolve issues efficiently. Collaborative tools like bug-tracking systems and test management software enable seamless communication and provide a centralized platform to track and fix defects.

Project Management Department

Effective collaboration and communication are the lifeblood of the project management department. Project managers must ensure all stakeholders are aligned, deadlines are met, and resources are allocated optimally. Regular meetings, status updates, and progress reports keep everyone informed and ensure project goals are achieved. Collaboration tools like project management software, task tracking systems, and communication platforms facilitate effective communication and enable project managers to manage teams and tasks efficiently.

User Experience (UX) Design Department

Collaboration and communication are crucial in the UX Design Department as designers work closely with developers and stakeholders to create user-friendly software interfaces.

Regular meetings, design reviews, and feedback sessions help understand user requirements, iterate designs, and deliver intuitive user experiences. Collaboration tools like design prototyping software and user testing platforms aid in effective communication and seamless collaboration between designers, developers, and users.

In conclusion, collaboration and communication are the backbone of successful software development projects. Regardless of the department, teamwork and effective communication are essential for achieving project goals, delivering high-quality software products, and meeting customer expectations. By fostering a collaborative culture, utilizing the right tools, and maintaining open lines of communication, the software industry department can ensure successful software project delivery.

3. Tools and Technologies Used in Software Development

Many tools and technologies facilitate and streamline software development in today's rapidly evolving software industry. These tools play a critical role in enhancing productivity, ensuring quality, and meeting the ever-growing demands of end users. This section will share information on the essential tools and technologies used in software development departments across various industry domains.

One of the fundamental tools in software development is *an Integrated Development Environment (IDE)*, which provides a comprehensive platform for writing, debugging, and testing code. Popular IDEs include *Visual Studio*, *Eclipse*, and *Xcode*, each tailored to specific programming languages and environments. These IDEs offer features like code completion, version control integration, and debugging tools, enabling developers to write and maintain code efficiently.

Another vital technology in software development is version control, which allows multiple developers to collaborate on a codebase seamlessly.

Git, a distributed version control system, is extensively adopted in the industry due to its flexibility and robustness. Platforms like *GitHub* and *Bitbucket* provide hosting services for Git repositories, promoting effective teamwork and code-sharing.

Continuous integration and delivery (CI/CD) tools like *Jenkins* and *Travis are* extensively used to automate the software build and deployment. These tools enable developers to automatically build, test, and deploy software changes, reducing manual effort and ensuring a stable and reliable software release process.

In terms of testing, the software QA department relies on a range of tools like *Selenium* and *JUnit* for automated testing, ensuring that the software meets the required quality standards. Additionally, performance testing tools like *Apache JMeter* and load testing tools like *Gatling* help ensure that software applications can handle high traffic and perform optimally under stress.

For the user experience (UX) design department, prototyping tools like *Sketch* and *Adobe XD* are commonly used to create interactive mockups and wireframes. These tools allow designers to visualize and iterate on the user interface design, resulting in seamless and intuitive user experiences.

Other departments within the software industry, such as project management, technical support, sales and marketing, research and development, data analytics, cybersecurity, training, and documentation, also rely on specialized tools and technologies to carry out their respective functions effectively.

In conclusion, the software industry encompasses many departments, each utilizing specific tools and technologies to support their unique roles. Familiarizing yourself with these tools and technologies will give you a competitive edge and equip you with the necessary skills to succeed in the dynamic world of software development.

Software Dev. Dept. Structure - Generalized View

The job hierarchy in a software development department typically consists of the following levels:

Intern

A student or recent graduate gaining experience in software development. They typically work on small tasks under the supervision of more experienced engineers.

Entry-Level Software Engineer

An entry-level software engineer is a recent graduate with a bachelor's degree in computer science or a related field. They typically work on small to medium-sized projects and may be responsible for writing code, testing, and debugging.

Junior Software Engineer

Engineer with 1-3 years of experience in software development. They typically work on medium to large projects.

Senior Software Engineer

Engineer with 5+ years of experience in software development. They typically work on large projects and may be responsible for mentoring junior engineers, syncing with designing software architectures, and leading teams.

Principal Engineer

An Individual contributor with a deep understanding of software engineering principles and practices. They typically work on cutting-edge projects and may be responsible for defining new technologies and methodologies.

Software/Technical Architect

A Senior software engineer with extensive experience designing and architecting software systems. They typically work on large, complex projects and may be responsible for setting the overall technical direction of the project.

Technical Lead

A Technical lead oversees a team of developers, guiding them through the development process, reviewing code, and ensuring the project is on track. They also collaborate with other groups and stakeholders to align technical decisions with business goals.

Development Manager

Development Managers manage multiple software projects, allocate resources, set project priorities, and ensure the development process runs smoothly. They also work closely with other departments to coordinate cross-functional efforts.

Engineering Director/VP of Engineering

This role involves strategic leadership, where individuals oversee the entire software development department. They set the long-term technical vision, manage budgets, and make decisions that impact the organization's technological direction.

Chief Technology Officer (CTO)

At the highest level, the CTO is responsible for the company's overall technology strategy. They drive innovation, evaluate emerging technologies, and ensure that the technology decisions align with the organization's business objectives.

It's important to note that the software development field is dynamic, and roles can evolve based on the organization's size, industry, and project complexity. Also, some companies might have additional functions, such as Quality Assurance Engineers, DevOps Engineers, and Product Managers, collaborating closely with the development team to create a well-rounded software development ecosystem.

In addition to these technical roles, several non-technical functions are essential to the software development process, such as:

Product Manager

A professional responsible for a product's success. They work with various stakeholders, including engineers, designers, marketers, and sales representatives, to define the product vision, roadmap, and features. They also track the product's performance and make adjustments as needed.

Project Manager

A professional who leads the team and manages the planning, organizing, and overseeing the execution of a project. They work with stakeholders to ensure the project is delivered timely, within the defined budget, and to the highest quality standards.

Business Analyst

A professional who assists organizations in comprehending their business requirements and transforming them into effective solutions. BAs work with various stakeholders, including business users, IT professionals, and project managers. They use their communication, analysis, and problem-solving skills to bridge the gap between business and technology.

All of these roles play an essential part in the software development process, and the success of any software project depends on the team members' effective collaboration.

Software Development Interview Questions

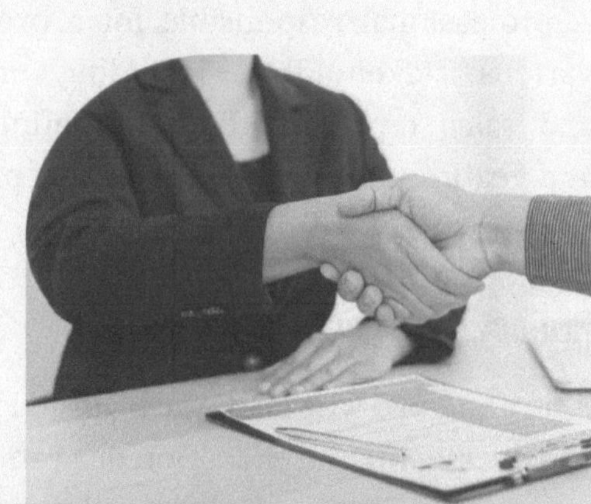

1. Please share your experience working on a difficult software development project and elucidate how you successfully tackled the challenges.
2. What are the different stages of the software development lifecycle (SDLC)?
3. What distinguishes functional requirements from non-functional requirements?
4. What is object-oriented programming (OOP), and what are its key principles?
5. What is data structure and algorithm design? Explain with an example.
6. Have you used cloud computing platforms like AWS or Azure?

Chapter 7

Quality Assurance Department

Overview

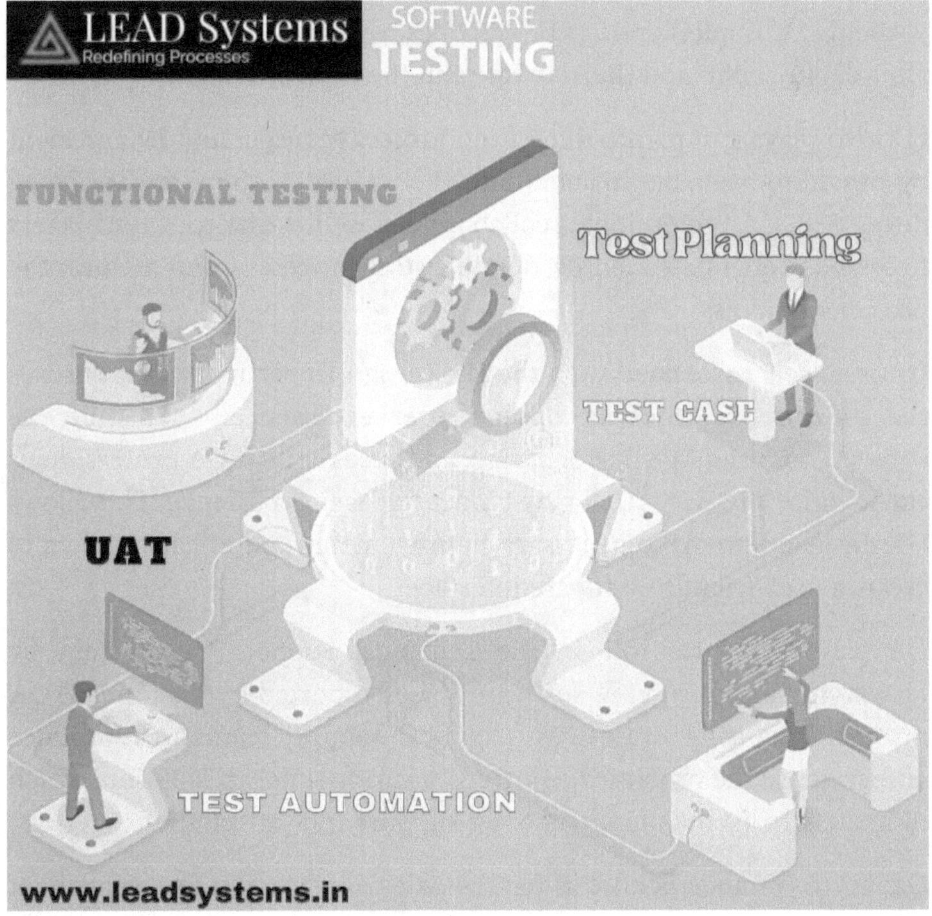

In the fast-paced world of software development, the importance of ensuring the quality of software products cannot be overstated. This section delves into the significance of Quality Assurance (QA) in software development and its impact on various departments within the software industry.

Quality Assurance is a crucial aspect of the software industry as it guarantees that the developed software meets the highest quality standards. The role of QA professionals is pivotal in identifying and addressing any defects, bugs, or errors in the software, thus ensuring its reliability and functionality. Software products may suffer from poor performance, security vulnerabilities, and customer dissatisfaction without QA. Implementing QA practices reduces the cost of fixing bugs after deployment, and the software can function seamlessly.

QA also plays a dynamic role in the Project Management Department by providing valuable insights into the quality of the software being developed. QA professionals collaborate closely with project managers to establish quality standards, define testing processes, and monitor the project's progress.

QA is closely associated with the UX Design Department as it ensures the software provides an optimal user experience. By testing the software for usability, performance, and accessibility, QA professionals can identify any issues that may hinder the user experience. This allows UX designers to make necessary improvements and enhancements to create a user-friendly software interface.

QA plays a critical role in the Technical Support Department by identifying and resolving software issues reported by customers. QA professionals collaborate with technical support teams to reproduce and diagnose the problems reported, ensuring timely resolution, which ultimately helps maintain customer support and satisfaction.

Quality Assurance is crucial for the Sales and Marketing Department as it ensures that the promoted software products meet the promised quality standards. QA professionals work closely with sales and marketing teams to validate product claims, conduct pre-release testing, and provide accurate information about the software's features and capabilities.

In conclusion, Quality Assurance is a fundamental component of software development and various departments within the software industry. QA ensures that software products meet the highest standards of quality, resulting in customer satisfaction, reduced costs, and improved efficiency.

Types of Testing in Quality Assurance

Quality assurance (QA) is crucial in the software industry, ensuring that software products meet the highest quality and performance standards. Testing is a critical component of QA, which involves evaluating the software for defects, errors, and functionality issues. This section will explore the various types of testing in quality assurance.

Functional Testing

This type of testing focuses on verifying whether the software meets the specified functional requirements. It involves testing individual features and functions to ensure they work as intended.

Performance Testing

Performance testing evaluates the software's performance under different conditions and measures its response time, scalability, and stability. It helps identify bottlenecks and performance issues that may arise during actual usage.

Security Testing

Security testing assesses the software's ability to protect data and prevent unauthorized access. It includes vulnerability assessments, penetration testing, and evaluating encryption and authentication mechanisms.

Usability Testing

Usability testing examines the software's user-friendliness and ease of use. It involves observing users performing specific tasks and collecting feedback to identify usability issues.

Compatibility Testing

Compatibility testing ensures the software functions correctly across different platforms, operating systems, browsers, and devices. It verifies that the software is compatible with the intended environment.

Regression Testing

Regression testing ensures that new changes or updates do not introduce defects or impact existing functionality. It involves retesting previously tested features to ensure they still work as expected.

Acceptance Testing

Acceptance testing determines whether the software meets the customer's requirements and is ready for deployment. It involves validating the software against predefined acceptance criteria.

Load Testing

Load testing evaluates the performance of the software under various load conditions, such as high user traffic or data loads. It helps identify performance bottlenecks and assess system capacity.

Stress Testing

Stress testing involves subjecting the software to extreme conditions to evaluate its stability and performance limits. It helps identify how the software handles unexpected loads or adverse circumstances.

Smoke Testing

Smoke testing is a quick, preliminary test to ensure that the critical functionalities of the software are working correctly before proceeding with further testing. It helps identify significant defects early on.

These are just some of the many types of testing in quality assurance. Each type of testing serves a unique purpose and ensures the software's overall quality and dependability. By understanding these testing types, students can gain insights into the diverse aspects of quality assurance and make informed decisions when pursuing a career in the software industry.

Challenges and Strategies for Success

The Quality Assurance (QA) Department plays a critical role in certifying the quality of products and services. However, the QA Department also faces some challenges, including:

Incomplete or Inaccurate Requirements

The QA team cannot test what they do not know, so it is essential to have clear and complete requirements. However, conditions are often incomplete or inaccurate, which can lead to defects in the product.

Communication Breakdowns

The QA team must communicate effectively with other stakeholders, such as the development team, the product owner, and the customers. However, communication breakdowns can occur, leading to misunderstandings and defects.

Limited Resources

The QA team may not have the resources to do their job effectively, such as enough time, staff, or money. This can lead to defects being overlooked or not being fixed.

Changing Requirements

Requirements often vary during development, making it difficult for the QA team to keep up. This can lead to defects being missed or not being fixed.

Technical Challenges

The QA team may face technical challenges like complex systems or new technologies. These challenges can make it difficult to test the product effectively.

Balancing Speed and Quality

The QA team must balance delivering the product on time with ensuring its quality. This can be a tricky balancing act, leading to defects being overlooked or not being fixed.

Despite these challenges, some strategies can be used to succeed in the QA Department. These strategies include:

Developing a QA Plan

The QA plan should document the QA process, including the activities that will be performed, the required resources, and the timeline for completing the activities.

Documentation

The QA team should document the product's requirements, test cases, and results. This documentation will help ensure the product is thoroughly tested, and defects are tracked and fixed.

Risk-Based Testing

The QA team should focus on testing the areas of the product that are most likely to have defects. This can be done by using risk analysis techniques.

Test Early and Often

The QA team should start testing the product early in development. This will help identify and fix defects early before they become more expensive.

Review and Inspection

The QA team should inspect the product's documentation, code, and other artifacts. This will help to identify potential defects before they are released to production.

Test Automation

The QA team can use test automation to automate repetitive testing tasks. This can free the QA team to focus on more complex testing tasks.

Maintain a Traceability Matrix

The traceability matrix will help ensure all test cases are linked to the product's requirements. This will help to ensure that the product is tested thoroughly.

User Acceptance Testing

The QA team should conduct User Acceptance Testing (UAT) to ensure the product meets the users' needs.

By following these strategies, the QA Department can overcome its challenges and successfully ensure the quality of products and services.

Best Practices for Quality Assurance

Quality Assurance is critical to software development and ensuring that software products meet the highest quality and functionality standards. This section aims to provide students with an understanding of the best practices that should be followed in the Quality Assurance Department within the software industry.

Test Planning and Strategy

A well-defined test plan and strategy are essential for adequate quality assurance. Students should learn how to identify the scope of testing, set clear objectives, and define the target audience. Additionally, they should understand how to prioritize testing activities based on risk assessment.

Test Case Design

Students should be familiar with various techniques for designing test cases, such as boundary value analysis, equivalence partitioning, and error guessing. They should also understand the importance of creating comprehensive and reusable test cases that cover all possible scenarios.

Test Execution and Reporting

Proper execution of test cases and accurate reporting of test results are crucial. Students should learn how to execute tests systematically, document any defects found, and communicate the results effectively to the development team.

Test Automation

Automation can significantly enhance the efficiency and effectiveness of quality assurance processes. Students should gain knowledge of different automation tools and techniques and understand when and how to implement them appropriately.

Continuous Integration and Continuous Testing

In modern software development, continuous integration and testing have become standard practices. Students should know the benefits of integrating testing activities into the development process and understand how to set up a continuous testing environment.

Collaboration and Communication

The Quality assurance department must collaborate closely with other departments. Students should learn effective communication strategies and techniques for working collaboratively with cross-functional teams.

Industry Standards and Regulations

Students should be familiar with industry standards and regulations for software quality assurance. They should understand the importance of compliance and learn how to incorporate these standards into their testing processes.

Continuous Learning and Improvement

Quality assurance professionals should embrace continuous learning and improvement. Students should be encouraged to stay updated with the latest trends, tools, and techniques in quality assurance and seek opportunities for professional growth.

By understanding and implementing these best practices for quality assurance, students can contribute to delivering high-quality software products and play a vital role in the company's success.

Quality Assurance Dept. Hierarchy – Generalized View

The job hierarchy in the quality assurance (QA) department in a software department typically follows this order:

Junior QA Engineer/Software Tester

This is an entry-level position in QA. Junior QA Engineers are responsible for performing manual tests and identifying bugs. They may also be responsible for creating user test cases and test plans.

Senior QA Engineer/Software Tester

Senior QA Engineers have more experience and knowledge than junior QA Engineers. They are responsible for leading and mentoring junior QA Engineers and developing and executing more complex test cases.

Test Architect

Test Architects design and develop test frameworks and automation tools. They also work with other QA Engineers to develop and execute test plans.

QA Lead/Test Lead

QA Leads manage a team of QA Engineers. They ensure that the team is following the QA process and that the quality of the software is being maintained.

QA Manager/Test Manager

QA Managers are responsible for the overall QA function in a company. They set QA policies and procedures and work with other departments to ensure the software's quality is met.

Director of Quality

The Director of Quality is responsible for the overall quality of the company's products and services. They work with their stakeholders to ensure quality is built in.

The job hierarchy may vary depending on the size and structure of the company. In smaller companies, there may be less hierarchy, with one person responsible for all aspects of QA. Larger companies may have more order layers, with each level having more specialized responsibilities.

Here are some of the critical skills and qualities that are important for success in a QA role:

- Strong analytical and problem-solving skills
- Attention to detail and desire to improve the quality of software
- Ability to work independently and as part of a team
- Excellent communication skills
- Ability to learn new technologies quickly

Quality Assurance Department Interview Questions

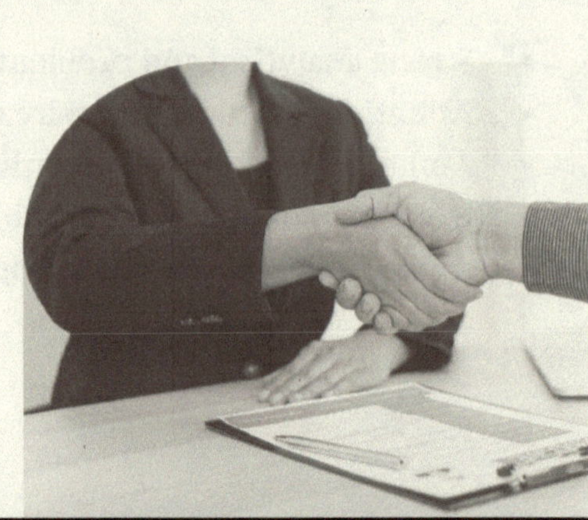

1. What is the Software Development Life Cycle (SDLC), and where does QA fit?
2. What are the different types of software testing?
3. What is the difference between black-box testing and white-box testing?
4. What is a test case, and how do you write a good test case?
5. What is a Bug report?

Chapter 8

Project Management Department

Overview

www.leadsystems.in

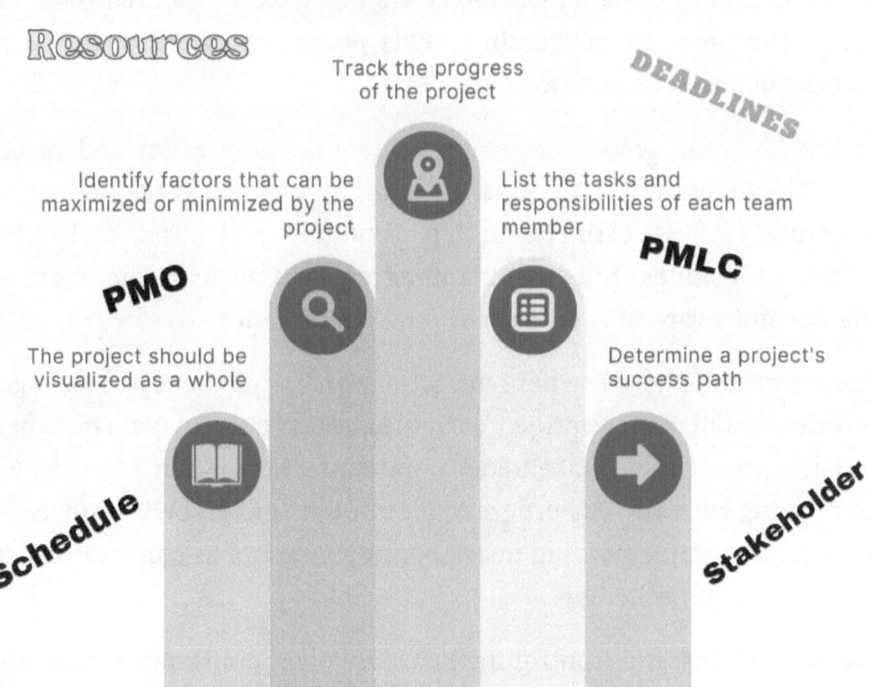

The Project Management Office (PMO) in the software industry provides centralized support for project management activities across the organization. The project management life cycle provides a systematic approach to effectively plan, execute, monitor, and control projects from start to finish. Whether you are a student aspiring to work in a software industry department or a professional seeking to enhance your project management skills, understanding the project management life cycle is essential.

Project Management Life Cycle (PMLC)

The Project Management Life Cycle comprises five key phases: Initiation, Planning, Execution, Monitoring and Controlling, and Closure. Let's delve into each step to gain a comprehensive understanding.

The Initiation phase marks the commencement of a project. During this phase, project managers identify the project's objectives, stakeholders, and scope. They conduct feasibility studies, assess potential risks, and define the project's deliverables. This phase sets the foundation for successful project execution.

In the Planning phase, project managers develop a detailed project plan. They identify the necessary resources, create a Work Breakdown Structure (WBS), estimate project timelines and costs, and define project milestones. Effective planning ensures all team members are aligned and aware of their roles and responsibilities.

The Execution phase is where the actual work begins. Project managers coordinate and manage project activities, assign tasks to team members, and ensure effective stakeholder communication. Their role involves monitoring the project's progress, identifying and resolving any issues or risks, and implementing necessary adjustments to confirm that the project stays on schedule.

The Monitoring and Controlling phase involves continuous evaluation of project performance. Project managers compare progress against the planned objectives, monitor resource utilization, and implement corrective actions when necessary. They also manage stakeholder expectations and ensure project deliverables meet quality standards.

Finally, the Closure phase signifies the completion of the project. Project managers conduct a thorough review to identify lessons learned and best practices. They obtain feedback from stakeholders and document the project's successes and challenges. This stage offers insights for upcoming projects and enhances the teams' efficiency.

In conclusion, the Project Management Life Cycle is a crucial framework that guides the successful execution of software development projects. By comprehending and applying this life cycle, the productivity and efficacy of software industry departments can be significantly improved. By following a systematic approach from initiation to closure, project managers can ensure that projects are delivered on time, within budget, and with the highest quality standards. Whether you aspire to work in project management, development, quality assurance, or any other software industry department, mastering the project management life cycle will provide you with a solid foundation for success.

Key Functions of the Project Management Dept

The critical functions of a project management team are crucial for ensuring the successful planning, execution, and completion of projects. Here are the essential tasks of a project management team:

Project Planning

The team initiates the project by defining its scope, objectives, and deliverables. They create a detailed project plan outlining tasks, timelines, and resource requirements. This plan should detail the tasks, deadlines, and resources needed to complete the project. This involves monitoring the project's progress against the plan and identifying potential risks or problems.

Resource Management

This involves allocating and managing resources such as people, materials, and equipment to ensure they are available when needed throughout the project.

Risk Management

Recognizing, evaluating, and mitigating risks is critical. A strategic mindset would be valuable in anticipating potential issues and developing a risk mitigation plan.

Budgeting and Cost Control

Project managers must establish budgets, track expenditures, and control costs to ensure the project remains within financial constraints.

Communication Management

The role of Communication Management is to ensure that the right messages are communicated to the right people in the right way at the right time. This can be a cumbersome task, as it requires understanding the needs of different audiences, the best channels to reach them, and the most effective way to convey the message. Project managers must ensure clear and timely communication among team members, stakeholders, and clients.

Task Tracking and Reporting

Keeping track of progress and performance is crucial. Project management tools and regular reporting help in this regard.

Stakeholder Management

Building positive relationships with stakeholders, including clients, team members, and vendors, is vital for project success.

Change Management

Being open to adapting the project plan when necessary is critical. Project managers should have a process for handling, reviewing, and prioritizing the requests and assessing the impact on the project.

Closure and Evaluation

Once the project is completed, the team should conduct a closure review to evaluate its success, document lessons learned, and ensure a smooth transition to ongoing operations or the next project phase.

Challenges of PMO

Indeed, addressing challenges and implementing effective strategies in project management is crucial for success.

Unclear goals and Objectives

If the project goals are vague, successfully planning and executing the project will be challenging.

Scope Creep

The tendency for projects to grow in size and complexity over time. This can lead to budget issues and create delays.

Unrealistic Deadlines

Too tight deadlines can lead to stress and burnout among team members and increase the risk of mistakes.

Lack of Communication

Communication is vital for successful project management. If there is poor communication between team members, stakeholders, or other project participants, it can lead to problems.

Team Conflict

Conflict can arise between team members for various reasons, such as personality clashes, disagreements about work priorities, or feeling like they are not being heard.

Resource Constraints

Not having enough resources, such as time, money, or people, can make it challenging to complete a project successfully.

Risk Management

Unmanaged risks can lead to problems.

Technology Issues

Technology can be a great asset to project management, but it can also be a source of problems. If the technology is unreliable or does not meet the project's needs, it can lead to delays or mistakes.

These are a few challenges that project managers may face. By being aware of these challenges, project managers can prepare a mitigation plan and increase the chances of project success.

Strategies for the Success of PMO

Clear Project Charter

Start with a well-defined project charter that outlines goals, objectives, scope, and stakeholders. Ensure everyone understands the project's purpose.

Project Management Software

Utilize project management software to efficiently track tasks, timelines, and resource allocation. This can help in real-time collaboration and progress monitoring.

Stakeholder Engagement

Engage stakeholders throughout the project's lifecycle. Regularly communicate progress and involve them in critical decisions.

Risk Mitigation

Continuously assess risks and have contingency plans. Regular risk reviews will help you stay proactive in addressing potential issues.

Agile Methodology

Consider using Agile methodologies if the project requirements are likely to change. It allows for flexibility and adaptability.

Training and Development

Invest in the training and development of your project team. Ensure they have the skills and knowledge needed for the project's success.

Document Everything

Maintain detailed project documentation, including project plans, status reports, and meeting minutes. This provides a clear historical record.

Lessons Learned

At the end of each project, conduct a lessons-learned session to identify what went well and what needs improvement for future projects.

Continuous Improvement

Encourage a culture of constant improvement. Use feedback from each project to refine your project management processes.

It is significant to remember that effective project management often requires a combination of structured methodologies and flexible strategies that can be tailored to meet the exceptional requirements of the project and the organization.

PMO Department Job Hierarchy – Generalized View

The job hierarchy in a project management team can differ depending on the project's size and complexity, but some roles are typically found in most groups. The job hierarchy in a project management team is essential for ensuring that the project is managed effectively.

The different roles have different levels of responsibility and authority, which helps to ensure that tasks are delegated and coordinated effectively. The job hierarchy also helps to create a clear line of communication between the different members of the team.

Here are some of the critical responsibilities of each of the roles in the project management hierarchy:

Project Manager

- Define the project scope
- Develop a project plan
- Execute the project plan
- Communicate with stakeholders
- Manage risks
- Resolve problems

Senior Project Manager

- Mentor and train junior project managers
- Oversee multiple projects or a large, complex project
- Ensure that projects are delivered timely, within budget, and meet quality standards

Director PMO

- Oversee the project management function within an organization
- Ensure that projects are aligned with the organizational vision and mission.
- Develop and implement project management standards and procedures.

Project Coordinator

- Provide administrative support to the project manager
- Schedule meetings
- Track progress
- Prepare reports

Team Leader

- Ensure goals and objectives are met
- Assign tasks
- Resolve problems
- Communicate with team members

A project management team's job hierarchy is dynamic and ever-changing. As the project progresses, the roles and responsibilities of the different members of the group may change. However, the overall goal of the job hierarchy is to ensure that the project is managed effectively and that the project team is successful.

Project Management Interview Questions

1. Tell me about your experience in managing and leading cross-functional teams.
2. How do you define success for a project, and what metrics do you use to measure it?
3. Can you describe a time when you had to handle an unexpected challenge during a project and how you dealt with it?
4. How do you keep all stakeholders informed and up-to-date throughout the project lifecycle?
5. Can you explain your risk management approach and how you identify and minimize potential risks?

Chapter 9

Technical Support Department

Overview

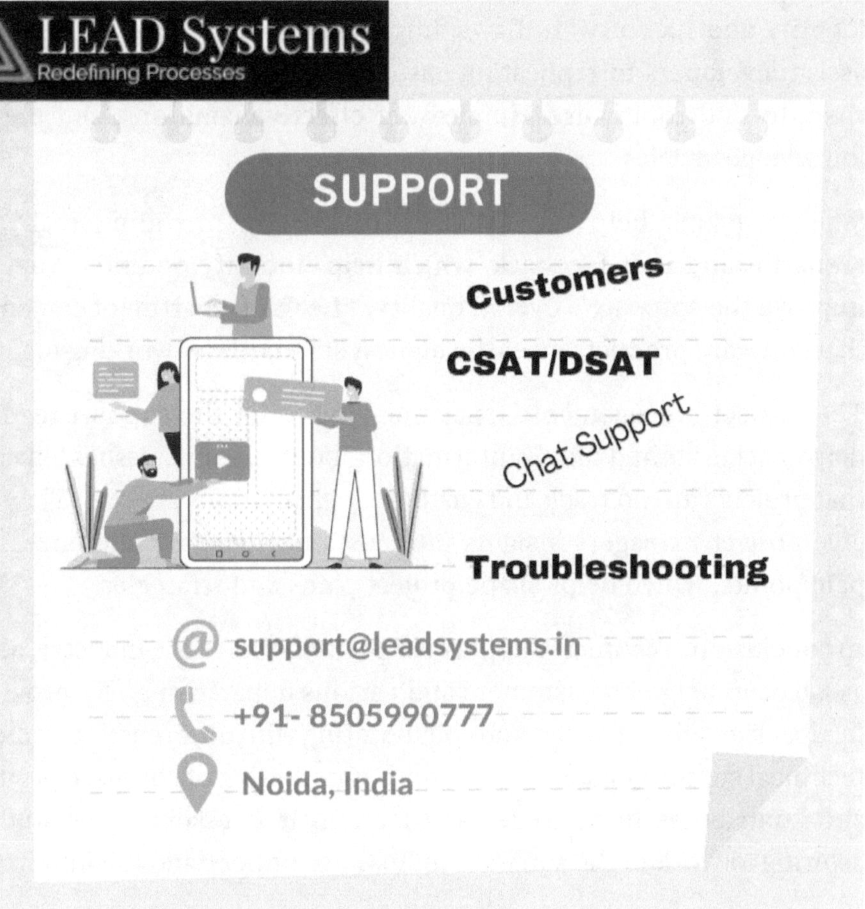

Technical Support is critical in the software industry, ensuring customers can use and troubleshoot software products effectively. In this chapter, we will explore the importance of this department and its impact on various departments within the software industry.

The Technical Support Department acts as a bridge between customers and other departments, such as software development, quality assurance, and user experience design. Ensuring customer satisfaction and the smooth functioning of software products, they hold a vital position.

The Technical Support provides valuable feedback and insights regarding bugs, glitches, and user experience issues. This helps developers to identify and fix software flaws, improving product quality. They also assist developers in replicating customer-reported problems, enabling them to find root causes, implement effective solutions, and prepare knowledge articles.

Support teams help the QA Department by providing real-world scenarios and user feedback, which helps identify potential bugs and improve the software's overall quality. The QA Department can ensure that software products meet the highest standards by working together.

The Project Management Department relies on the support teams to deliver accurate and timely information about customer issues, ensuring that projects are on track and customer expectations are met. They also give project managers insights into customer needs, preferences, and pain points, which helps shape project plans and strategies.

In conclusion, Technical Support is vital in the software industry, acting as a liaison between customers and various departments. By providing feedback, resolving issues, and collaborating with different departments, technical support ensures the smooth functioning of software products and contributes to customer satisfaction. It is essential for students aspiring to work in the software industry to understand the importance of technical support and its impact on different departments within the industry.

Key Functions of the Support & Maintenance Team

The software industry's technical support and maintenance teams are vital in ensuring software products function correctly and meet users' needs.

The Technical Support team is responsible for assisting users of software products. This includes answering questions, troubleshooting problems, and providing training. The team may be involved in a variety of activities, such as:

- Answering phone calls and emails from users
- Logging and tracking support tickets
- Analyzing and troubleshooting problems
- Providing remote assistance to users
- Creating and updating documentation
- Providing training to users

The Maintenance team is responsible for keeping software products up and running. This includes fixing bugs, adding new features, and improving performance. The maintenance team may be involved in a variety of activities, such as:

- Analyzing software logs to identify and fix bugs
- Developing and testing new features
- Optimizing software performance
- Conducting security audits
- Deploying software updates

The Technical Support and Maintenance teams collaborate closely to guarantee the reliability and user-friendliness of software products. They play a critical role in the success of any software company.

Here are some additional details about the key functions of each team:

Technical support

The Technical Support team is the first line of defense for users having problems with a software product. Users may contact them via phone, email, or chat. The technical support team will typically try to resolve the problem via phone or email. If the problem is more complex, the technical support team may need to escalate the issue to the maintenance team.

Maintenance

The Maintenance team is responsible for fixing bugs, adding new features, and improving the performance of software products. They may also be responsible for developing and testing new software releases. The maintenance team collaborates with the development team to guarantee the accurate implementation of new features without causing any negative impact on performance. Here is an example of how the technical support and maintenance teams might work together to resolve a problem:

"A user calls the technical support team with a problem. The technical support team troubleshoots the issue and determines that it is a bug in the software. The technical support team then escalates the case to the maintenance team. The maintenance team works with the Software development team to fix the bug and releases a new patch. The technical support team then informs the user of the latest software update and helps them to install it."

In conclusion, the Technical Support and Maintenance teams are essential for the success of any software company. Providing timely and accurate assistance to users helps to ensure that software products are used effectively and efficiently. By fixing bugs and adding new features, they help to keep software products up-to-date and user-friendly.

Critical Aspects of this Department

Troubleshooting and Problem-Solving Techniques

Whether you're working in software development, quality assurance, project management, user experience design, technical support, sales and marketing, research and development, data analytics, cybersecurity, or training and documentation, identifying and resolving issues quickly and effectively is crucial.

This section will provide valuable techniques and strategies to enhance your troubleshooting and problem-solving skills. By mastering these techniques, you'll be better equipped to handle challenges that arise in your department and contribute to the overall success of your organization.

First and foremost, developing a systematic approach to troubleshooting is essential. The process includes dissecting intricate problems into smaller, more achievable components. Pinpointing the fundamental reason behind an issue saves time and resources by avoiding unnecessary solutions. Documenting your troubleshooting process can also help you track your progress and identify patterns in recurring problems.

Another valuable technique is using diagnostic tools and software to identify and analyze problems by providing detailed error logs, performance metrics, and system diagnostics. Please familiarize yourself with the tools specific to your department and learn how to interpret their outputs effectively.

Effective communication, preparing, and sharing knowledge articles are vital when troubleshooting and problem-solving. Collaborate with your team members, share information, and seek their input. Often, a fresh perspective can lead to innovative solutions. Keep your stakeholders informed about the progress and potential solutions to demonstrate your commitment to resolving the issue.

Furthermore, updating industry trends and advancements can significantly benefit your troubleshooting skills. Attend relevant conferences, workshops, and webinars to enhance your knowledge and gain insights from industry experts. Engage in continuous learning and seek opportunities to sharpen your technical skills.

Lastly, don't be afraid to experiment and be creative in your problem-solving approach. Sometimes, unconventional solutions can lead to breakthroughs. Embrace a growth mindset and be open to new ideas and perspectives.

Incorporating these troubleshooting and problem-solving techniques into your daily work will make you a valuable asset to your software industry department. Your ability to quickly identify and resolve issues will increase productivity, customer satisfaction, and overall success.

Customer Support and Service Level Agreements

In the fast-paced and ever-evolving software industry, providing exceptional customer support is crucial for the success of any department. Be it any department, understanding the importance of customer support and service level agreements (SLAs) is essential.

Customer support goes beyond simply resolving customer issues and answering questions. It is about building solid relationships with customers and ensuring their satisfaction throughout their journey with your software product or service. By offering timely and required support, you not only enhance customer loyalty but also improve the reputation and credibility of your department.

Service level agreements are established to ensure consistent and reliable customer support. An SLA is a contract between your department and the customer outlining the service level they can expect to receive. It includes details such as response times, resolution times, availability of support channels, and escalation processes.

Defining the terms and expectations in an SLA sets the groundwork for a positive customer experience. It allows your department to manage customer expectations and prioritize support requests based on their urgency and impact on the customer's business operations.

When designing SLAs, it is essential to consider your department's unique needs and characteristics. For instance, in software development, SLAs may focus on bug fixes and feature requests, while in quality assurance, SLAs may concentrate on the time taken to validate and report issues.

To effectively meet SLA commitments, collaboration among various departments is essential. This collaboration ensures that customer issues are escalated and resolved efficiently, regardless of the department responsible for the resolution. Effective communication and coordination across teams contribute to a seamless support experience for the customer.

Moreover, continuously monitoring and analyzing customer support metrics, such as response time and customer satisfaction/ dissatisfied customer (CSAT or DSAT) scores, enables your department to identify areas for improvement. Regularly reviewing SLAs, making necessary adjustments based on customer feedback, and changing business requirements ensures that your department stays agile and responsive to customer needs.

In conclusion, customer support and service level agreements are vital for any software industry department. By prioritizing customer satisfaction, establishing clear SLAs, fostering collaboration, and continuously improving support processes, your department can deliver exceptional customer experiences and contribute to the overall success of your software service.

Challenges and Strategies for Success

The Support and Maintenance (S&M) Department is responsible for keeping software applications running smoothly and efficiently after they have been released to customers. This can be challenging, as software applications are constantly evolving and changing.

Some of the critical challenges faced by S&M departments include:

Cost Control

Support and Maintenance can be a significant expense for businesses, accounting for up to 60% of the total cost of software development. Developing cost-effective S&M strategies that do not compromise support quality is essential.

Impact Analysis

When changes are made to software, it is essential to consider the impact of those changes on the rest of the system. This can be a complex task, as software applications are often interconnected.

Corrective Changes

When software defects are found, they must be fixed quickly and efficiently. This could be a tedious job, as faults can be difficult to identify and reproduce.

Program Understanding

As software applications become more complex, it can be difficult for engineers to understand how the code works. This can make it difficult to troubleshoot problems and make changes.

Here are some strategies for success in the S&M department:

Invest in Automation

Automation can reduce the cost and complexity of the support and maintenance department. Many tools can automate defect tracking, change management, and testing tasks.

Use a Proactive Approach

Rather than waiting for problems to occur, the support team should take a proactive approach to maintenance. This includes monitoring software for defects and proactively fixing them before they cause user problems.

Build a Strong Relationship with Users

The Support team should build a strong relationship with users by creating a feedback mechanism so users can report problems efficiently and fix them quickly.

Use a Continuous Learning Approach

The software industry constantly evolves, so the support and maintenance department must stay alert to the latest technologies and best practices.

The team can overcome challenges and provide high-quality customer support by following these strategies.

Customer S& M Dept Hierarchy – Generalized View

The job hierarchy in the support and maintenance department in the software industry typically follows this order:

Support Technician

This is an entry-level position in the support department. The technicians provide basic troubleshooting and support to customers. They may also be responsible for data entry, documentation, and other administrative tasks.

Senior Support Technician

Senior support technicians have more experience and knowledge than support technicians. They are responsible for more complex troubleshooting and support issues. They may also train and mentor new buddies on the floor.

Support Engineer

Support engineers deeply understand the software product and the underlying technologies. They are responsible for resolving the most complex support issues. They may also develop and implement new support processes and procedures.

Floor Manager

Responsible for the overall management of the support department. They are responsible for setting goals, allocating resources, and ensuring the department meets the customers' needs.

Director

The Director is responsible for the overall strategy and direction of the support department. They work with other departments to ensure the support department is aligned with the overall business goals.

The job titles and responsibilities may vary depending on the size and structure of the organization. However, the general job hierarchy is the same.

In addition to the technical skills required for these positions, support and maintenance professionals also need strong communication and customer service skills. They must effectively communicate with customers to understand their problems and provide solutions. They must also be able to work under pressure and meet deadlines.

If you are interested in a career in support and maintenance, there are a few things you can do to prepare.

First, you should develop your technical skills by taking courses, attending workshops, or getting certified in the software products you want to support.

Second, you should develop your communication and customer service skills. You can do this by volunteering, taking classes, or getting a job in a customer-facing role. Finally, it would help if you networked with people in the software industry. This will help you learn about job opportunities and open doors for you.

Technical Support Interview Questions

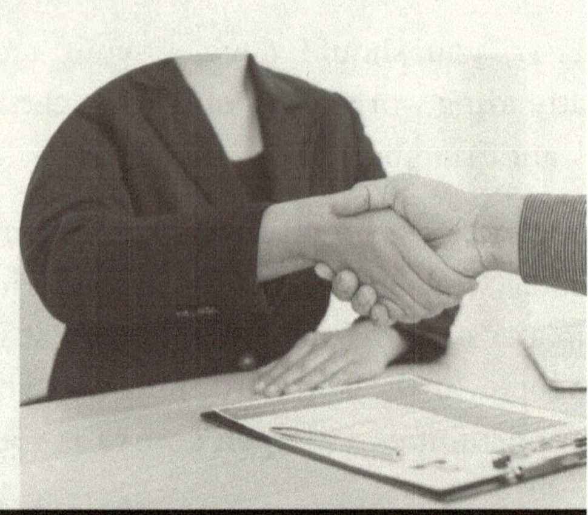

1. What is your troubleshooting process?
2. What is your experience with our company's products and services?
3. How do you handle difficult customers?
4. How do you stay up-to-date on the latest technologies and software?
5. What is your experience with remote support tools and techniques?

Chapter 10

Sales and Marketing Departments

Overview

SALES & MARKETING

LEAD GENERATION

Quota

www.leadsystems.in

BOOK ONLINE

The Sales and Marketing Department for software products generates leads, nurtures prospects, and closes deals. They work closely with the product development team to understand the features and benefits of the software product and then develop marketing and sales strategies to reach the target audience. This chapter will give students a comprehensive overview of the various stages of bringing a software product to market.

Key Functions of the Sales and Marketing Team

Selling Products and Generating Revenue

Some of the specific responsibilities of the sales and marketing department for software products include:

Market Research

The Sales and Marketing team must understand the target market to create effective campaigns and pitches. They do this by conducting market research, which involves gathering data on the target audience's demographics, needs, and pain points.

Lead Generation

Once the target market has been identified, the Sales and Marketing team must generate leads. This can be done through various channels, such as online advertising, content marketing, and attending industry events.

Lead Qualification

The Sales and Marketing team must qualify leads to identify those most likely to become customers. This involves evaluating the lead's interest in the product or service, their budget, and their decision-making authority.

Once leads have been qualified, the sales and marketing team must nurture them to keep them engaged and interested in the product or service. This can be done by sending them educational content, providing customer support, and inviting them to participate in webinars or events.

Closing Deals

The ultimate goal of the sales and marketing team is to close deals and convert leads into customers. This involves having a robust sales process and effectively communicating the product or service's value to the customer.

Upselling and Cross-Selling

Once a customer has been acquired, the Sales and Marketing team can upsell and cross-sell other products or services. This can help to increase the average customer lifetime value and boost revenue.

The Sales and Marketing Department for software products is as important as other departments. You are creating something, so you need to sell it, too. By effectively generating leads, nurturing prospects, and closing deals, they can help to ensure that the company's software products are successful in the market.

Here are some additional tips for the Sales and Marketing department for software products:

Focus on the Customer

The Sales and Marketing team should always keep the customer in mind. What are their needs? What are their pain points? How can the software product solve their problems? The Sales and Marketing team can develop more effective marketing and sales strategies by understanding the customer.

Use Data to Drive Decisions

The Sales and Marketing team should use data to gauge their improvement and measure the effectiveness of their campaigns. This data helps identify what is working and what is not and make necessary adjustments to their strategies.

Stay Up-to-Date on Trends

The software industry is constantly evolving, so the sales and marketing team needs to stay alert to the latest trends. This will help them develop marketing and sales strategies relevant to their target audience.

In conclusion, understanding the software product market is essential for anyone aspiring to work in the software industry. Each department plays a vital role in bringing a software product to market, and collaboration between these departments is critical to success. By grasping the intricacies of each stage, students can gain a well-rounded understanding of the software industry and prepare themselves for a successful career in their chosen niche.

Challenges and Strategies for Success

The software industry is rapidly changing and competitive, which poses several challenges for Sales and Marketing teams. Here are some of the most common challenges:

The High Cost of Customer Acquisition

Software products can be expensive to develop and market, so sales and marketing teams must be very efficient to acquire new customers.

The Long Sales Cycle

The sales cycle for software products can take months or even years to close a deal. This can be a challenge for sales teams, which must be patient and persistent to win business.

Complexity

Software products can be complex and difficult to understand, making it challenging for sales and marketing teams to communicate their value to potential customers.

Technical Expertise

Sales and marketing teams in the software industry must understand the products they sell. This is essential to answer customer questions and provide accurate information.

The Competition

The software industry is very competitive, with many companies contending for the same customers. This means that Sales and Marketing teams keep innovating and find new ways to stand out.

Despite these challenges, there are several strategies that Sales and Marketing teams can use to achieve success in the software industry. Here are some of the most effective methods:

Identify the Right Target Audience

It is important to focus marketing efforts on the right target audience. This means understanding your ideal customers' needs and pain points and creating content and messaging that resonates with them.

Use Data-Driven Marketing

Sales and marketing teams should use data to track the results of their campaigns and make necessary adjustments. This will help ensure they get the most out of their marketing budget.

Create Valuable Content

Creating valuable content is an effective strategy to captivate and involve prospective customers. By producing top-notch content tailored to your specific audience, you can establish yourself as a knowledgeable authority in your industry, fostering trust among potential customers.

Build Relationships

Sales and Marketing teams should focus on building relationships with potential customers. This can be accomplished by attending industry events, connecting with influential individuals, and delivering exceptional customer service.

Be Patient and Persistent

It takes time and effort to succeed in the software industry. Sales and marketing teams should be patient and persistent and never give up on a potential customer.

Be Creative and Innovative

The software industry constantly changes, so sales and marketing teams must be creative and imaginative. This means thinking out of the box and developing new ways to reach and engage potential customers.

By following these strategies, sales and marketing teams can overcome the challenges of the software industry and achieve success.

Critical Aspects in the Sales & Marketing Department

Market Research and Competitive Analysis

In the fast-paced world of the software industry department, staying ahead of the competition is crucial for success. To thrive in this ever-evolving landscape, it is essential for students aspiring to work in the software industry department to understand the importance of market research and competitive analysis.

Market Research gathers and analyzes information about potential customers, target markets, and industry trends. This process aids software companies in recognizing opportunities, evaluating demand, and making well-informed choices regarding product development and marketing approaches. Through market research, students can gain valuable insights into customer preferences, identify unmet needs, and stay updated with the latest trends and technologies.

Competitive analysis, on the other hand, involves evaluating the strengths and weaknesses of competitors and assessing their strategies and market position. By reviewing the competitive landscape, the team can pinpoint areas where the market is lacking and create distinctive selling points for their software products or services.

In addition, competitive analysis helps determine the pricing, positioning, and marketing strategies to give their software company a competitive edge. Companies can benefit from market research and competitive analysis by understanding software users' common issues and identifying improvement areas. This knowledge helps them provide adequate and timely customer support, enhancing customer satisfaction and loyalty. Also, they can leverage market research and competitive analysis to identify emerging technologies, market trends, and customer needs. This knowledge helps them innovate and create software products that meet future market demands.

The Sales and Marketing Department for software products can use market research and competitive data analysis to identify target markets, develop marketing strategies, and position their products effectively. By understanding customer needs and competitor offerings, sales and marketing professionals can communicate the unique value of their software products and drive sales.

In conclusion, Market research and Competitive analysis play a vital role in the success of the software industry department.

Product Positioning and Pricing Strategies

Product positioning and Pricing strategies are two crucial marketing decisions that can significantly impact a company's success.

Product positioning is establishing a unique and recognizable image in consumers' minds. This can be done by highlighting certain features or benefits of the product or by comparing it to other products in the market. Product positioning aims to make the product stand out from the competition and appeal to a specific target market.

The Pricing strategy refers to determining the prices for goods and services. The choice of pricing strategies may vary depending on the nature of the product, the intended audience, and the company's objectives. There are several commonly used pricing strategies, including:

Cost-plus pricing

This strategy sets prices based on the product's cost and profit margin.

Market-based pricing

This strategy sets prices based on what the competition is charging.

Value-based pricing

This strategy sets prices based on the product's perceived value to the customer.

The best pricing strategy for a particular product will depend on several factors, including the cost of production, the competitive landscape, and the target market.

Product positioning and pricing strategies should be carefully considered together. The right combination of product positioning and pricing can help a company achieve its marketing goals and increase sales.

Here are some of the tips used in the industry for developing effective product positioning and pricing strategies:

Understand your target audience

The first step is understanding your target audience and their value in a product that will appeal to them.

Consider your competition

It's also important to consider your competition when developing your product positioning and pricing strategies. What are your competitors doing? How are they positioning their products? How are they pricing their products? By understanding your competition, you can develop strategies that will help you stand out from the crowd.

Use Market research

Market research can help you understand your target market, competition, and landscape. Market research can be valuable for developing effective product positioning and pricing strategies.

Be flexible

The market is constantly changing, so it's essential to be flexible with your product positioning and pricing strategies. If something isn't working, be willing to change it. Here are some additional examples of product positioning:

- **Apple**: Apple positions its products as stylish, innovative, and user-friendly.
- **Adobe**: Adobe positions its products as creative and user-friendly.
- **Nike**: Nike positions its products as high-quality, stylish, and performance-driven.
- **Starbucks**: Starbucks positions its coffeehouses as welcoming, comfortable, and stylish.

Carefully considering product positioning and pricing strategies can increase the chances of success in the marketplace.

Promotional Activities and CRM Solution

In today's competitive software industry, promotional activities and customer relationship management (CRM) are essential for the success of any department. Whether you are working in software development, quality assurance, project management, user experience design, technical support, sales and marketing, research and development, data analytics, cybersecurity, or training and documentation, understanding and implementing these strategies can significantly impact your department's growth and success.

Promotional activities and Customer Relationship Management (CRM) are two closely related concepts essential for any business that wants to succeed. Promotional activities are designed to attract new customers and generate sales, while CRM is focused on building relationships with existing customers and keeping them coming back for more.

When done effectively, promotional activities and CRM can work together to create a powerful marketing machine that drives growth and profitability. Here are a few ways to integrate promotional activities and CRM:

- Utilize CRM data for precise promotional targeting.. Using CRM software, you can effectively divide your customer base according to their demographics, interests, and purchase history. This valuable information can then be utilized to develop tailored marketing campaigns that will likely resonate with your intended audience.
- Personalize your promotions. Once you know your target audience, you can personalize your advertisements to their needs and interests. This can be done through email marketing, social media, or even direct mail.

- Make it easy for customers to redeem promotions. The last thing you want is for customers to have difficulty redeeming a promotion. Make sure your redemption process is easy to understand.
- Track the results of your promotions. It's essential to track the results of your promotional activities so you can see what's working and what's not. This information can be used to improve your future campaigns.
- Ensure customers can quickly contact you through multiple channels like phone, email, and social media.
- Respond to customer inquiries promptly. They always appreciate it when their concerns are addressed quickly and efficiently.
- Go above and beyond to meet customer expectations. This could mean offering a refund, sending a replacement product, or apologizing for a mistake.
- Personalize your customer interactions. Use the information you collect from CRM to address customers by name, remember their preferences, and offer relevant products or services.

Integrating promotional activities and CRM can create a more effective marketing strategy to help you grow your business and build stronger customer relationships. These tips can promote customer relationship management and create a positive customer experience. This will help you build loyalty and may increase your chance of upselling/cross-selling. On a personal note, I worked extensively on Salesforce (SFDC) CRM from the Admin and Development side. I have implemented both the Sales and Service cloud.

Sales & Marketing Dept Hierarchy – Generalized View

The job hierarchy in the Sales and Marketing Department in the software industry typically follows this pattern:

Marketing Coordinator

Marketing coordinators are responsible for supporting the marketing team with creating content, managing social media, and organizing events.

Marketing Manager

Marketing managers are responsible for leading and managing a team of marketing professionals. They also develop and execute marketing strategies and track the marketing team's performance.

Product Marketing Manager

Product marketing managers are responsible for developing and executing marketing strategies for specific products or services. They typically work closely with product managers to understand the product and target market.

Sales Development Representative (SDR)

SDRs generate leads for the sales team. They typically do this by cold calling, emailing, and networking.

Account Executive (AE)

AEs are responsible for closing deals with potential customers. They typically work with SDRs to qualify leads and develop and execute a sales strategy.

Territory/Inbound Sales

This level includes sales development representative (SDR), marketing coordinator, and marketing intern positions. These roles are responsible for lead generation, content creation, and social media management.

Group Sales Manager

This role is responsible for leading and managing teams of sales and marketing professionals. They also develop and execute sales and marketing strategies.

VP's

This level includes positions such as Vice President of Sales and Marketing. These roles are responsible for overseeing the entire sales and marketing function. They also develop and implement long-term sales and marketing plans.

Executives

Positions such as Chief Executive Officer (CEO) and Chief Operating Officer (COO) are responsible for the company's overall success. They also set the vision and strategy for the sales and marketing function.

The job structure within this department may differ based on the company's size and organizational framework. However, the general job titles and responsibilities remain the same. If you are interested in a career in sales or marketing, it is important to understand the different job titles and duties to find the proper role for you.

Sales & Marketing Interview Questions

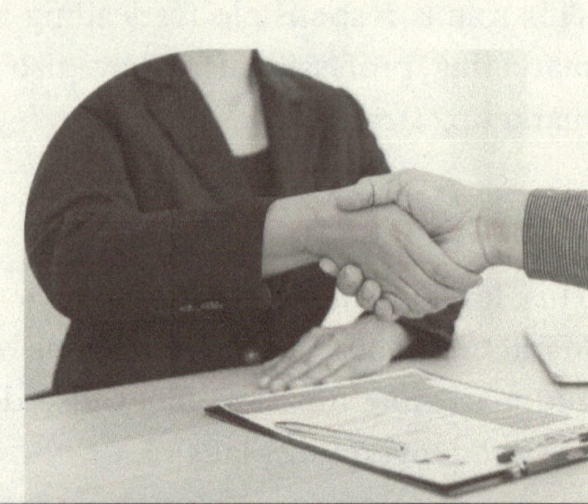

1. Tell me about when you overcame a challenge to close a deal.
2. What is your experience with generating and nurturing leads?
3. Can you please share your experience developing and implementing marketing campaigns?
4. What is your experience with using CRM software?
5. Why are you interested in working for our company?

Chapter 11

Research and Development Department

Overview

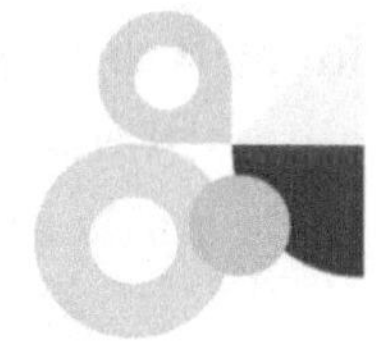

Research & Development

RedefiningProcesses.txt

```
(function repeat() {
eat();
sleep();
love_yourself();
repeat();
})();
```

#Motivation #Passion #Challenges

Prototyping

Cloud Computing

ARTIFICIAL INTELLIGENCE

Innovation

POC

www.leadsystems.in

A Research and Development (R&D) Department is a group of people within a company responsible for researching and developing new ideas, testing prototypes, services, and technologies, and bringing new products to market. It allows software companies to:

Drive Innovation

Software companies can create fresh and inventive products and services that cater to their customers' requirements by researching and staying updated on the latest trends and technologies.

Improve Existing Products and Services

R&D can also be used to improve current products and services by identifying and addressing areas for improvement. This approach allows software companies to maintain a competitive edge and expand their market share.

Ensure Quality and Reliability

R&D can also be used to ensure the quality and reliability of software products by identifying and fixing potential bugs and errors. This can help to improve the UX (user experience) and reduce the risk of development recalls.

Reduce Time to Market

Moreover, conducting Research and Development (R&D) assists in minimizing the time required to introduce new products and services to the market by identifying and resolving potential obstacles early.

Gain a Competitive Edge

By investing in R&D, software companies can gain a competitive edge over their rivals. This is because R&D allows software companies to develop new products and services that are unique and differentiated from those of their competitors.

In today's fast-paced and ever-changing software industry, R&D is more important than ever. Software companies that fail to invest in R&D will likely be left behind by their competitors.

Here are some specific examples of how R&D has been used to benefit the software industry:

Artificial Intelligence (AI)

AI is an expanding field that can bring revolutionary changes in various industries, including software. Research and development (R&D) is crucial in AI's advancement, enabling researchers to delve into novel ideas and technologies.

Cloud Computing

Cloud computing is another rapidly growing field transforming the software industry. R&D is essential for developing cloud computing, as it allows researchers to create new and innovative ways to deliver software and data to users.

The Development of Mobile Apps

R&D is necessary to develop new and innovative mobile apps. It allows researchers to explore new ways to use mobile devices and to create unique and engaging user experiences.

R&D is essential for the continued growth and innovation of the software industry.

Key Functions of the R&D Team

- Conducting research and development of new software products and technologies. This includes identifying new market opportunities, researching emerging technologies, and developing new software products and features.

- Designing and developing new software features and functionality. This involves working with product managers and other stakeholders to understand user needs and designing and developing software that meets those needs.
- Testing and debugging software to ensure quality and performance. This includes unit, integration, and system testing to ensure the software is bug-free and performs as expected.
- The process of optimizing software focuses on enhancing its performance and efficiency. This entails identifying and resolving areas within the software that can be improved to achieve faster execution and reduce resource consumption.
- Safeguarding software from vulnerabilities and attacks involves incorporating security mechanisms, like encryption and authentication, to shield the software from unauthorized entry and malicious assaults.
- Documenting software for easy understanding and maintenance. This involves creating clear and concise documentation that explains how the software works and how to use it.

The R&D department plays a critical role in the software industry, as it is responsible for developing new and innovative software that keeps businesses competitive. By investing in R&D, companies can stay ahead of the competition, improve their products and services, and create new market opportunities.

Sharing some specific examples of R&D projects in the software industry:

- Developing a new operating system that is more secure and efficient
- Creating a new programming language that is easier to learn and use
- Designing a new algorithm that can solve a complex problem faster

- Developing a new software application that can improve business operations
- Creating a new security feature that can protect against cyberattacks

The R&D department is essential in every software company as it serves a vital role. By dedicating resources to research and development, companies ensure an ongoing innovation process, developing unique products and services that meet their customers' needs.

Critical Aspects of the R&D Department

Innovation and Idea Generation

In today's fast-paced software industry, innovation and idea generation are crucial for the success of any department. Innovation goes beyond creating new products or features; it also includes finding inventive answers to current problems and enhancing processes. As a student aspiring to work in the software industry, it is essential to understand the significance of innovation and idea generation in your future career.

Establishing a culture that promotes and acknowledges creativity is a practical approach to nurturing innovation. This can be accomplished by fostering a supportive, cooperative work atmosphere that embraces ideas and facilitates brainstorming sessions. As a student, you can enhance your innovative thinking abilities by actively engaging in group projects, participating in problem-solving activities, and staying informed about cutting-edge technology.

Idea generation involves gathering information, analyzing data, and brainstorming solutions in a structured process. Involving all relevant stakeholders from different departments is crucial to ensure diverse perspectives and insights. As a student, you can practice idea generation by actively seeking feedback from peers and mentors and attending industry events and conferences.

Additionally, innovation and the generation of ideas heavily rely on technology. The software industry departments have gained access to immense amounts of data thanks to the progress in AI, ML, and big data analytics. This data can effectively identify patterns, trends, and lucrative opportunities. For students, acquiring the technical skills required to use these technologies in data analytics and cybersecurity to remain competitive in the ever-changing software industry is crucial.

In conclusion, innovation and idea generation are vital for the success of any software industry department. Students can position themselves as valuable assets in their future careers by fostering a culture of creativity, actively engaging in idea-generation processes, and staying up-to-date with the latest technologies.

Prototyping and Proof of Concept (POC)

Prototyping and proof of concept (POC) are essential steps in product development. They can help you validate your idea, test your assumptions, and get user feedback. However, there is a difference between the two.

Proof of concept is a demonstration that your idea is technically feasible. It shows that you can build something that works using the chosen technology. A POC is typically a rough prototype with limited functionality. It is not meant to be a polished product but to prove that the underlying concept is sound.

Prototyping is creating a working product model, which is used to test different designs, features, and interactions. Prototypes can be made from various materials and can be as simple or complex as needed. The goal of prototyping is to create a realistic representation of your product so that you can get user feedback and make necessary changes before you launch your final product.

When to Use a POC

It would help to use a POC when working with new or emerging technologies. A POC can help you to get buy-in from stakeholders and investors, and it can also help you to identify any potential challenges that you may face in development.

When to Use a Prototype

This is often the case when working with a complex product or when you are unsure what the final product should look like. Prototypes can help you get user feedback and make necessary changes before you launch your final product.

Which is Better?

There is no one-size-fits-all answer to this question. The approach will differ depending on the requirements. A prototype is an excellent option to test different designs, features, and interactions.

In many cases, using a POC and a prototype is helpful. The POC can help you get buy-in and identify challenges, while the prototype can help you test different designs and get user feedback.

Prototyping and proof of concept are valuable tools in product development. They can help you validate your idea, test your assumptions, and get user feedback. You can choose the right approach for your project by understanding the differences.

Intellectual Property Protection and Tech Transfer

In today's rapidly evolving digital landscape, Intellectual Property (IP) protection and technology transfer have become crucial aspects of the software industry. As students aspiring to work in various software industry departments, understanding these concepts is essential for ensuring the success and sustainability of software products and services. This section will delve into the significance of intellectual property protection and technology transfer, providing valuable insights for students across different niches within the software industry.

Intellectual property protection is the legal safeguarding of intangible assets, such as software, inventions, designs, or trademarks. It aims to provide exclusive rights to the creators or owners, encouraging innovation and preventing unauthorized use or infringement. Students in software development need to comprehend the importance of respecting existing intellectual property rights while creating new software solutions. They should learn how to navigate copyright, patent, and trademark laws to ensure the legality and originality of their work.

Moreover, the Quality Assurance Department ensures that software products comply with intellectual property regulations. Conducting thorough audits and checks, they help identify any potential infringements or vulnerabilities, thereby safeguarding the organization's IP rights.

Regarding technology transfer, students across various departments must understand the process of sharing or licensing technology from one organization to another. The Project Management Department is critical in facilitating technology transfer by ensuring smooth knowledge transfer between teams and maintaining effective communication channels.

The Technical Support Department is responsible for addressing customer queries and resolving issues related to software products. They must be well-versed in IP protection to guide customers on legal usage and customization of software. Similarly, the Sales and Marketing Department must be knowledgeable about IP protection to promote and sell software products while adhering to legal boundaries.

Research and Development Department drives innovation within the software industry. Understanding IP protection is vital for researchers to secure their inventions and discoveries, fostering a culture of creativity and advancement.

Furthermore, the Data Analytics Department handles vast amounts of sensitive data. They should be aware of IP protection regulations to ensure the security and privacy of intellectual property during data analysis and interpretation.

Lastly, the cybersecurity department protects software products and services from unauthorized access and theft. They must employ robust security measures to safeguard intellectual property from cyber threats and breaches.

In conclusion, Intellectual Property protection and technology transfer are crucial pillars of the software industry. Understanding these concepts is paramount for students aspiring to work in different software industry departments. By comprehending IP protection regulations and facilitating seamless technology transfer, students can contribute to the growth and success of the software industry while upholding the integrity and legality of software products and services.

Challenges and Strategies for Success

The software industry is fast-paced and constantly evolving, so R&D departments face several challenges. Some of the most common challenges include:

Competing Priorities

R&D teams are often asked to balance short-term goals with long-term innovation. This cannot be easy, as it requires careful planning and prioritization.

A Large Gap Between R&D and the Customer Expectations

R&D teams can sometimes be disconnected from customer needs when developing products. This can lead to the development of products that are not in demand or that do not meet customers' needs.

Underestimating the Importance of Success Metrics

R&D teams need clear success metrics to measure their progress and make necessary adjustments. Without clear metrics, knowing if R&D efforts are successful can be difficult.

Here are some strategies for overcoming these challenges and achieving success in the R&D department:

Align R&D with Business Goals

R&D teams should be aligned with the company's overall business goals. This means understanding the company's target market, competitive landscape, and long-term vision.

Focus on Customer Needs

R&D teams focus on understanding the customer's needs. This is achieved via. Surveys, interviews, and user research.

Use Agile Development Methodologies

Agile development methodologies can help R&D teams to be more responsive to change and to deliver products more quickly.

Use Data-Driven Decision-Making

R&D teams should use data to make project decisions. This data can come from customer surveys, user testing, and other sources.

Empower the Team

R&D teams should be empowered to make decisions and take risks. This will help them to be more innovative and to deliver better products.

Create a Culture of Innovation

Innovation should be encouraged and rewarded in the R&D department. This can be done by providing opportunities for experimentation and celebrating successes.

Invest in Training and Development

R&D teams need the skills and knowledge to succeed. This means providing them with training in new technologies and methodologies.

Collaborate with Other Teams

R&D teams should collaborate with other teams within the company, such as product management, marketing, and sales. This will ensure that products are developed to meet the needs of customers and the business.

Be Patient

R&D is a long-term process. It takes time to develop new products and technologies. R&D teams need to be patient and persistent to achieve success.

The R&D Department can overcome challenges and succeed in the software industry by following these strategies.

R&D Department Hierarchy – Generalized View

The job hierarchy in the R&D department of the software industry typically consists of the following levels:

Entry-level includes research assistant, software intern, and software developer positions require a bachelor's degree in CS, software engineering, or a related field. They are typically involved in working on small projects or tasks under the supervision of more experienced engineers. Duties may include writing code, debugging, and testing software.

Mid-level includes software engineer II, software architect, and technical lead positions. These positions typically require a master's degree in CS, software engineering, or several years of experience in software development. These positions involve more responsibility and independence. Engineers at this level may be responsible for leading small teams, designing and implementing software systems, or conducting research.

Senior-level positions include principal software engineer, software engineering manager, and software architect. These positions typically require a Ph.D. in CS, software engineering, or a related field or many years of experience in software development. These engineers deeply understand software development and are often responsible for mentoring and training junior engineers. They may also be involved in strategic planning and decision-making.

Executive level includes positions such as vice president of engineering, chief technology officer, and chief product officer. These positions typically require a Ph.D. in CS, software engineering, or many years of experience in a software development role. They are responsible for setting the department's vision, mission, and strategy.

The job titles and responsibilities may differ from company to company, but the general job hierarchy is the same. The higher the level, the more responsibility and experience the position requires.

Research and Development Interview Questions

1. Tell me about a time you had to solvc a complcx problem.
2. What are your areas of expertise in software development?
3. What is your experience with research and development?
4. What methods do you use to keep yourself informed about the most recent trends and technologies in software development?
5. What are your career goals for 5-10 years?

Chapter 12

Data Analytics Department

Overview

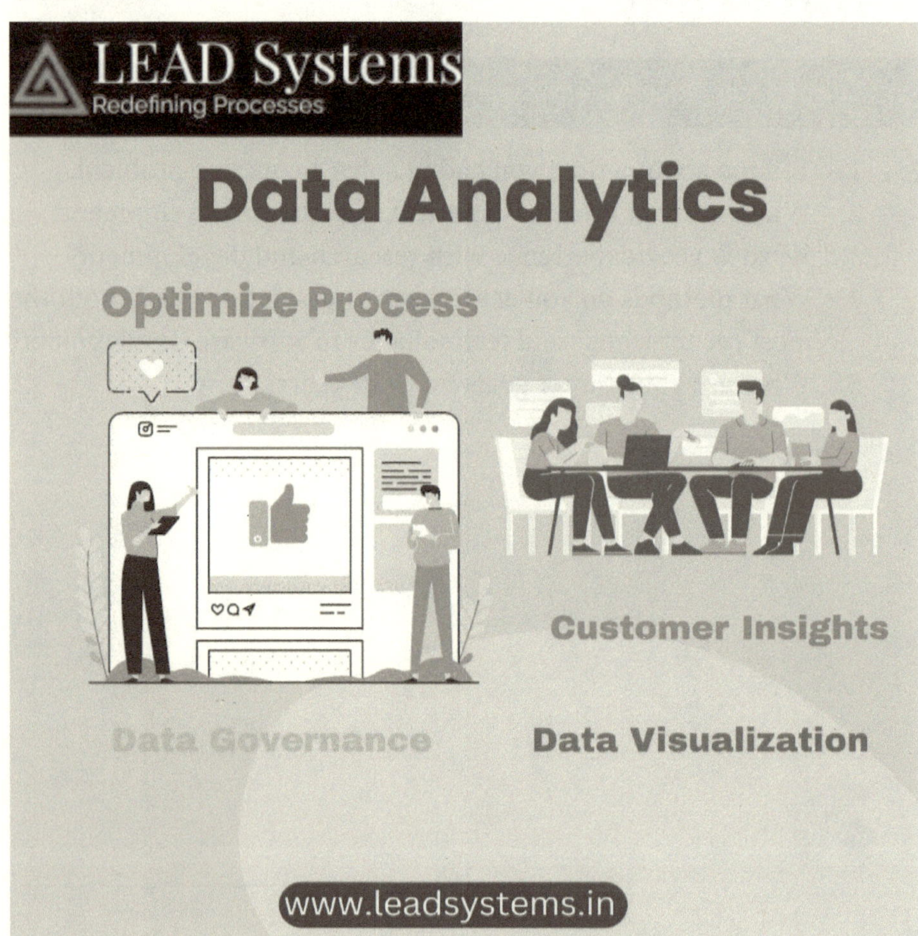

Data Analytics is becoming increasingly important in the software industry. Data analysis allows software companies to gain valuable insights into their customers, products, and operations. This information can then be used to improve decision-making, optimize processes, and develop new products and services.

Here are some of the specific ways that data analytics is being used in the software industry:

Customer Insights

Data Analytics can be used to understand customer behavior, preferences, and pain points. This information can then improve the user experience of software products and services. For example, It can personalize recommendations, identify customer churn, and target marketing campaigns.

Product Development

Data Analytics can identify new product opportunities, test, and iterate on product features, and measure the success of new products. For example, It can be used to track user engagement with different product features, identify bugs, and measure the impact of marketing campaigns on product adoption.

Operational Efficiency

Data Analytics can identify areas where software processes can be improved. This information can then be used to automate tasks, reduce costs, and improve the overall efficiency of software operations. For example, It can identify bottlenecks in the software development process, track software systems' performance, and optimize resource use.

Security and Compliance

Data Analytics can identify and mitigate security risks and ensure regulation compliance. For example, It can monitor user activity, detect suspicious behavior, and identify potential data breaches.

Data Analytics is a tool that can significantly improve the software industry. By collecting, analyzing, and interpreting data, software companies can gain valuable insights to help make better decisions, improve products and services, and operate more efficiently.

Here are some additional benefits of using data analytics in the software industry:

Increased Revenue

By understanding customer behavior and preferences, software companies can develop products and services that are more likely to be adopted by users. This can lead to increased revenue.

Reduced Costs

Data analytics can be used to identify areas where costs can be reduced. For example, data analytics can be used to automate tasks, optimize the use of resources, and identify potential areas for cost savings.

Improved Decision-Making

Access to data-driven insights allows software companies to make informed decisions about various aspects of their products. This can lead to improved business outcomes.

Enhanced Competitive Advantage

Software companies can gain a competitive advantage using data analytics to understand the market and its competitors better. This can help them attract new customers, grow their market share, and increase their profits.

As the amount of data generated by software continues to grow, the importance of data analytics will only increase. Software companies that can effectively use data analytics will be well-positioned to succeed in the years to come.

Key Functions of the Data Analytics Team

Data Analytics plays a critical role in empowering businesses to pinpoint opportunities for enhancing their operational effectiveness and output, but they typically include the following:

Data collection and preparation involves gathering data from various sources, cleaning and transforming it into a format that can be analyzed, and ensuring it is high quality.

Data analysis entails employing statistical and machine learning methods to uncover patterns and trends within the data, enabling predictions about future results.

Data visualization involves creating charts, graphs, and other visuals to communicate the data analysis findings to stakeholders.

Reporting involves summarizing and communicating the data analysis findings to stakeholders clearly and concisely.

Data governance ensures that the data is used responsibly and ethically and complies with all applicable regulations.

The team must remain informed about the latest data analytics techniques and technological advancements to ensure constant improvement and consistently enhance their skills and abilities.

Challenges and Strategies for Success

Here are some of the challenges and strategies for the success of a data analytics team:

Lack of Data Quality

Data is the foundation of data analytics, so the data must be accurate, complete, and consistent. However, data quality can be challenging, especially in large organizations with complex data systems.

Skills Shortage

There is a growing demand for data analysts, but the supply of skilled professionals is not keeping pace. This can make finding and hiring the right people for the job difficult.

Lack of Resources

Data Analytics can be resource-intensive, requiring investment in technology, infrastructure, and personnel. This can be a challenge for small businesses or organizations with limited budgets.

Cultural Resistance

Some organizations may resist change and be unwilling to use data to make decisions. This can make it difficult to implement data analytics successfully.

Data Security

Data Analytics can involve collecting and analyzing sensitive data, so protecting this data from unauthorized access is essential.

Strategies for Success

Establish a Clear Data Governance Framework

This will help collect, manage, and use data consistently and ethically.

Invest in Data Quality

This includes cleaning, formatting, and integrating data from multiple sources.

Develop a Data-Driven Culture

Creating an environment where data is valued and used to make decisions.

Train Employees on Data Analytics

To ensure that everyone in the organization understands the value of data and how to use it.

Use the Right Tools and Technologies

Various tools and technologies are available to support data analytics. Picking the precise ones for your organization will depend on your specific needs.

Partner with Experts

You can partner with a third-party vendor if you do not have the in-house expertise to manage your data analytics program.

By addressing these challenges and implementing the right strategies, you can create a data analytics team that successfully achieves your organization's goals.

Key Aspects of the Data Analytics Department

Data Collection and Warehousing

In the fast-paced world of the software industry, data collection and warehousing play a crucial role in driving decision-making and shaping the future of organizations. As students aspiring to be part of various software industry departments, understanding the importance of data and how it is collected and stored is paramount. This section will delve into the core concepts of data collection and warehousing, providing a solid foundation to thrive in the software industry.

Data collection refers to systematically gathering and evaluating data related to significant variables, enabling organizations to gain insights and make informed decisions. Data collection in the software development department can involve tracking user behavior, analyzing system performance, and monitoring application usage patterns. The quality assurance department collects data to identify and resolve software defects and ensure product quality.

The Project Management Department uses data collection to track progress, identify bottlenecks, and make data-driven decisions to achieve project objectives. The User Experience (UX) Design Department collects data to understand user preferences, behaviors, and pain points, enabling them to create intuitive and user-friendly software interfaces.

Data collection is not limited to the development and design department. The Technical Support Department uses data to diagnose and resolve customer issues efficiently, ensuring customer satisfaction. The Sales and Marketing Departments of software product companies utilize data to focus on the appropriate audience, tailor marketing campaigns to individuals, and evaluate the success of their approaches.

Once data is collected, it needs to be stored and organized for efficient retrieval and analysis. This is where data warehousing comes into play. Data warehousing involves the process of aggregating data from various sources into a centralized repository, often referred to as a data warehouse. The research and development department relies on data warehousing to store large volumes of experimental data for analysis and future reference.

The Data Analytics Department heavily relies on data warehousing to extract valuable insights, identify trends, and make data-driven predictions. The Cybersecurity Department utilizes data warehousing to detect and investigate security breaches and identify patterns of potential threats.

The Training and Documentation Department uses data warehousing to store and organize training materials, user guides, and other resources for easy access and knowledge sharing.

In conclusion, data collection and warehousing are critical software industry components. Regardless of the department you choose to pursue, understanding the processes and importance of data collection and data warehousing will empower you to make informed decisions, drive innovation, and contribute to the success of your organization.

Data Visualization and Reporting

Data Visualization and Reporting are two closely related concepts essential for businesses of all sizes. Data Visualization transforms data into visual representations like charts, graphs, and maps. This makes understanding complex data sets and identifying trends and patterns easier. On the other hand, reporting is the process of collecting and presenting data in a way that is easy to understand and use.

Data Visualization and Reporting can be used for a variety of purposes, including:

Understanding Data

Data Visualization can help businesses to better understand their data by making it easier to see trends, patterns, and outliers. This information can then be used to make better decisions about the business.

Communicating Data

Data Visualization can transmit data clearly and concisely to others. This can help share data with stakeholders, customers, or employees.

Making Decisions

Data Visualization can be used to make better decisions by providing insights into data. This information can identify opportunities, solve problems, and improve performance.

There are a variety of tools that can be used for data visualization and reporting, including:

Spreadsheets

Spreadsheets are simple and easy-to-use tools for Data Visualization and reporting. They can be used to create tables, charts, and graphs.

Data Visualization Software

Several programs offer more advanced features than spreadsheets. These programs can be used to create more complex visualizations and reports.

Business Intelligence (BI) Platforms

BI platforms are a suite of tools that can be used for Data Visualization, reporting, and analysis. They can integrate data from multiple sources. Tableau, Power BI, and Zoho are hot-selling BI tools available.

Data Visualization and Reporting are essential tools for businesses of all sizes. By using these tools, companies can better understand their data, communicate data to others, and make better decisions.

Predictive Analytics and Machine Learning

Predictive Analytics and Machine Learning are two powerful tools that can improve decision-making in the software industry.

Predictive Analytics uses historical data to classify patterns and trends to predict future outcomes. For example, predictive analytics can predict which customers are most likely to churn, which software features are most likely to be used, or which code changes are most likely to introduce defects.

ML is an artificial intelligence that allows software to learn without being explicitly programmed. ML algorithms can identify patterns in data and make predictions based on those patterns. For example, machine learning can classify software bugs, recommend products to customers, or personalize user experiences.

Predictive Analytics and machine learning can provide software companies with a wealth of insights to improve their products, services, and operations.

Here are some specific examples of how predictive analytics and ML are being used in the software industry:

Churn prediction

Predictive Analytics can identify customers at risk of churning, which can help software companies prevent those customers from leaving. *For example, Netflix uses predictive analytics to identify customers who are not watching as much content as they used to. Netflix then sends those customers personalized recommendations or offers discounts to keep them subscribed.*

Feature Prioritization

Predictive Analytics can prioritize software features based on their impact on customer satisfaction or revenue. *For example, Microsoft uses predictive analytics to prioritize features for its Office 365 suite. Microsoft's predictive models consider customer usage data, customer feedback, and competitor analysis.*

Defect Prediction

Machine Learning can be used to predict which software changes are most likely to introduce defects. This information can be used to arrange testing efforts and reduce the number of flaws that make it into production. *For example, Google uses ML to predict which lines of code are most likely to contain bugs. Google's machine learning models are trained on historical data, including data about past bugs.*

Recommendation Engines

Machine Learning can be used to create recommendation engines that recommend products, services, or content to users. *For example, Amazon uses ML to recommend products to prospects based on their previous purchases, browsing data, and ratings.*

Personalized User Experiences

Machine Learning can personalize user experiences by tailoring content, recommendations, and interactions to each user. *For example, Netflix uses machine learning to personalize the home screen for each user based on their viewing history and preferences.*

These are just a few examples of how predictive analytics and ML are used in the software industry. With these technologies advancing, we can expect even more pioneering ways to use them to improve software products and services.

Data Analytics Dept Hierarchy – Generalized View

The job hierarchy in a data analytics team typically consists of the following roles:

Junior Data Analyst

The Entry-level position is responsible for collecting, cleaning, and analyzing data. They may also be responsible for creating simple reports and visualizations. Junior analysts typically have a bachelor's degree in data science, statistics, or a related field.

Data Analyst

The Mid-level position is responsible for more complex data analysis tasks, such as building predictive models and developing data-driven solutions. May also be responsible for leading and mentoring junior analysts. Data analysts typically have master's degrees in data science, statistics, or related fields.

Senior Data Analyst

The Senior-level position leads and manages data analytics projects. May also be responsible for developing and implementing data governance policies and procedures. Senior data analysts typically have master's degrees in data science, statistics, or related fields.

Data Scientist

A hybrid role that combines the skills of a data analyst and a software engineer. Accountable for developing and deploying machine learning models to solve business problems. A data scientist typically holds a Ph.D. in data science/ statistics or has an extensive experience in this field.

Data Engineer

Accountable for building and maintaining the data infrastructure that supports data analytics. This includes data warehousing, data pipelines, and data security. Data engineers typically have a bachelor's degree in computer science or a related field.

Analytics Manager

Responsible for the overall management of the data analytics team. This includes setting goals, allocating resources, and evaluating performance. Analytics managers and directors usually hold a master's degree in business administration (MBA) specializing in data analytics.

Director of Analytics

Responsible for the strategic direction of the data analytics function. This includes developing and implementing data analytics initiatives and aligning data analytics with business goals. A director-level person usually has a Ph.D. in data science, statistics, or a related field and has extensive data analytics experience.

Specific roles and responsibilities may vary by organization. However, the positions listed above are common to most data analytics teams.

The job hierarchy in a Data Analytics team is important for ensuring that the team is adequately staffed and that the right people are responsible for the right tasks. It also helps to ensure that the team is aligned with the business goals and that the data analytics function is managed effectively.

Data Analytics Interview Questions

1. What is the data analysis process?
2. What are the different types of data analysis?
3. What are some of the challenges you face during data analysis?
4. What are some of your favorite data analysis tools and technologies?
5. Why are you interested in working as a data analyst?

Chapter 13

CyberSecurity Department

Overview

Cybersecurity is essential in every industry but especially critical in software. Software applications are increasingly used to store, process, and transmit sensitive data, making them prime targets for cyberattacks.

Here are some of the reasons why Cybersecurity is so vital in the software industry:

- In order to safeguard sensitive data, software applications often store private information such as financial data, personally identifiable information (PII), and intellectual property. If a data breach occurs, there is a potential danger of valuable information being stolen or disclosed, resulting in significant financial, legal, and reputational consequences for the software company.
- To maintain customer trust. The security of customers' data is becoming a growing concern. A data breach could damage a software company's reputation, making attracting and retaining customers difficult.
- To comply with regulations. Many industries are subject to rules requiring them to protect specific data types. A software company that does not adhere to these regulations may be fined or penalized.
- To protect intellectual property. Software companies often develop proprietary software that is their most valuable asset. A data breach could expose this intellectual property to competitors, giving them a significant advantage.
- To prevent business disruption. A cyberattack could disrupt a software company's operations, losing revenue and productivity.

In addition to these reasons, Cybersecurity is essential in the software industry because it can help improve software product quality. By implementing security best practices, software companies can create products that are more resistant to cyberattacks. This can help to protect users from data breaches and other security incidents.

Overall, Cybersecurity is an essential part of the software development process. By protecting their software applications, software companies can help safeguard their data, protect their customers, comply with regulations, and prevent business disruption.

Key Functions of the Cybersecurity Team

The critical functions of the Cybersecurity Department in the Software industry are:

Risk Assessment and Management

Identify and assess the risks to the software company's information assets. Create and execute strategies to minimize the impact of those risks.

Incident Response

Respond to security incidents, such as data breaches, malware attacks, and denial-of-service attacks. The objective is to reduce the consequences of security incidents and safeguard information assets' confidentiality, integrity, and availability.

Security Awareness and Training

Educate employees about cybersecurity risks and best practices. Help employees identify and report suspicious activity and protect their information assets.

Compliance

Ensure the software company complies with all cybersecurity regulations and standards. Protect the software company from legal penalties and reputational damage.

Vulnerability Management

Identify and mitigate vulnerabilities in the software company's systems and applications. Protect the software company from cyberattacks that exploit vulnerabilities.

Security Architecture and Engineering

Design and implement secure software systems and architectures. Protect the software company from cyberattacks by building security into the design of its systems and applications.

Security Operations

Monitor and maintain the software company's security infrastructure. Detect and respond to security threats promptly.

Challenges of Cybersecurity

Indeed, addressing challenges and implementing strategies for the success of the Cybersecurity Department in the software industry is crucial. Here are some key insights:

Evolving Threat Landscape

The cybersecurity landscape changes as new threats and attack vectors emerge frequently. Staying ahead of these threats can be challenging.

Talent Shortage

Finding and retaining skilled cybersecurity professionals is a common challenge. The demand for cybersecurity experts often outpaces the supply.

The Complexity of Software

As software becomes more complex, it becomes harder to secure. This complexity can create vulnerabilities that cybercriminals can exploit.

Compliance and Regulations

The software industry must comply with various data protection regulations, which can be challenging to navigate and adhere to consistently.

Advanced Persistent Threats (APTs)

APTs are sophisticated, long-term cyberattacks that can be hard to detect and mitigate.

Strategies for Success

Continuous Training and Education

Invest in ongoing training and education for your cybersecurity team. This enables employees to remain informed about the most recent threats and technologies.

Robust Risk Assessment

Regularly assess the organization's cybersecurity risks and vulnerabilities. Perform penetration testing and vulnerability assessments to uncover vulnerabilities within your software, thus identifying potential weak spots.

Implement Zero Trust Architecture

Assume that threats exist inside and outside the network and authenticate and authorize all users and devices. By doing this, the likelihood of insider threats is reduced.

Incident Response Plan

Create a comprehensive plan for incident response to promptly and efficiently address security incidents. Practice these response procedures through simulations.

Compliance and Governance

Establish robust governance frameworks to ensure compliance with relevant regulations. Stay informed about any modifications in data protection regulations and adjust your policies accordingly.

Collaboration and Information Sharing

Collaborate with industry peers and share information about emerging threats and vulnerabilities. Collective intelligence can help in staying ahead of cyber threats.

Security by Design

Embed security into the software development lifecycle. Implement secure coding practices and conduct regular security code reviews.

Threat Intelligence

Use threat intelligence sources to detect threats and vulnerabilities affecting your software.

Vendor Security Assessment

Assess the cybersecurity practices of third-party software and service providers to ensure they meet your security standards.

Regular Updates and Patch Management

Ensure that software and systems are regularly updated with the most recent security patches to address any identified vulnerabilities effectively.

Success in cybersecurity within the software industry requires a proactive and adaptive approach. By tackling these challenges head-on and incorporating these strategies, your Cybersecurity Department can enhance the overall security posture of your organization.

Significant Aspects of the Cybersecurity Department

Threats and Vulnerabilities in Software Systems

One of the most common threats faced by software systems is hacking. Hackers are constantly looking for software vulnerabilities to gain unauthorized access to sensitive information. They can steal personal data and financial information or even take control of the entire system. This poses a significant risk to the software industry department as it can lead to financial losses, reputational damage, and legal consequences.

Another major threat is malware, which includes viruses, worms, and trojans. Malware can infect software systems and cause various issues, such as data corruption, system crashes, and unauthorized remote access. Email attachments, malicious websites, or infected external devices could be the source. The department must be vigilant and apply robust security measures to detect and prevent malware attacks.

Data breaches are also a significant concern for software systems. With the increasing amount of sensitive data stored in software applications, the risk of unauthorized access or accidental data exposure has grown exponentially. This can result in severe consequences, including financial losses, regulatory penalties, and loss of customer trust. The department must prioritize data security and encryption to protect sensitive information.

Moreover, software systems are vulnerable to human errors, such as coding mistakes or misconfigurations. A minor issue can have significant consequences, including system failures or security breaches. Therefore, the Software Development and Quality Assurance

Department must follow best practices, such as code reviews, testing, and continuous monitoring, to minimize these vulnerabilities.

As technology evolves, new threats and vulnerabilities continue to emerge. The Cybersecurity Department plays a vital role in identifying and mitigating these risks. They conduct regular security audits, implement firewalls and intrusion detection systems, and educate employees about cybersecurity best practices.

In conclusion, the software industry department faces numerous threats and vulnerabilities that can compromise the functionality and security of software systems. It is essential for all departments, including Software Development, Quality Assurance, Project Management, and User Experience, to prioritize Cybersecurity and implement robust security measures to protect against hacking, malware, data breaches, and human errors. By ensuring the integrity and confidentiality of their software systems, software industry departments can safeguard sensitive data and retain the trust of their customers.

Importance of Cybersecurity Tools

Cybersecurity tools are essential for protecting organizations and individuals from cyber threats. These tools can help to prevent, detect, and respond to cyberattacks, and they can also help to recover from data breaches.

Here are some of the most critical cybersecurity tools:

Firewalls

A crucial network security tool that helps monitor and filter network traffic. Its primary function is to apply predetermined security rules to incoming and outgoing data. A firewall acts as a safeguarding barrier, creating a division between trusted and untrusted networks, such as the Internet.

Intrusion Detection Systems (IDS)

IDSs monitor network traffic for malicious activity. They can detect known attacks, as well as new and emerging threats.

Antivirus Software

Antivirus software scans files and applications for malware. It can also quarantine or delete infected files.

Encryption

It protects data from unauthorized access. Encryption tools protect data by scrambling it so it cannot be read without the correct key.

Incident Response Tools

Incident response tools help organizations to quickly and effectively respond to cyberattacks. They can collect evidence, contain the attack, and restore systems.

Identity and Access Management (IAM)

The systems control who has access to what resources and how to use them.

Here are some of the top cybersecurity tools in 2023:

- Palo Alto Networks Cortex XDR is a comprehensive security platform that provides threat prevention, detection, and response capabilities.
- CrowdStrike Falcon is an AI-powered, cloud-based endpoint protection platform that effectively detects and addresses threats.
- McAfee Total Protection is an antivirus and anti-malware solution that also provides features for web protection, firewalls, and parental controls.

- Bitdefender Total Security is another comprehensive antivirus and anti-malware solution with online privacy protection and password management features.
- Kaspersky Security Cloud is a security solution that protects devices, networks, and data.

In conclusion, Cybersecurity tools are essential to any organization's security strategy. Using multiple tools, organizations can help protect their systems, networks, and data from various threats.

Cyber Security Dept Hierarchy – Generalized View

The job hierarchy in a cybersecurity team can vary depending on the organization's size and structure, but some typical roles are found in most units. Here is a general overview of the job hierarchy in a Cybersecurity team:

Chief Information Security Officer (CISO)

The CISO is the highest-ranking cybersecurity professional in an organization. They are responsible for creating an overall Cybersecurity strategy at the organization level.

Vice President of Cybersecurity (VP Cybersecurity)

The VP of Cybersecurity reports to the CISO and oversees the cybersecurity team's day-to-day operations.

Director of Information Security (Director of InfoSec)

The Director of InfoSec reports to the VP of Cybersecurity and leads a team of cybersecurity engineers and analysts.

Cybersecurity Engineer

Cybersecurity Engineers design, implement, and maintain the organization's security infrastructure.

Cybersecurity Analyst

Analysts monitor the organization's network and systems for security threats. They also investigate security incidents and vulnerabilities.

Security Architect

Security Architects design and implement the organization's security architecture.

Security Awareness Trainer

Security Awareness Trainers educate employees about cybersecurity threats and best practices.

In addition to these typical roles, there are many other specialized cybersecurity roles, such as penetration testers, ethical hackers, and digital forensic analysts. The specific job titles and responsibilities will vary depending on the organization's needs.

Here are some of the factors that can affect the job hierarchy in a cybersecurity team:

- The size and complexity of the organization.
- The industry that the organization operates in.
- The level of risk that the organization faces.
- The budget is available for cybersecurity.

As the organization grows and the level of risk increases, the job hierarchy may need to be adjusted to ensure enough resources to protect the organization's assets.

Cybersecurity Interview Questions

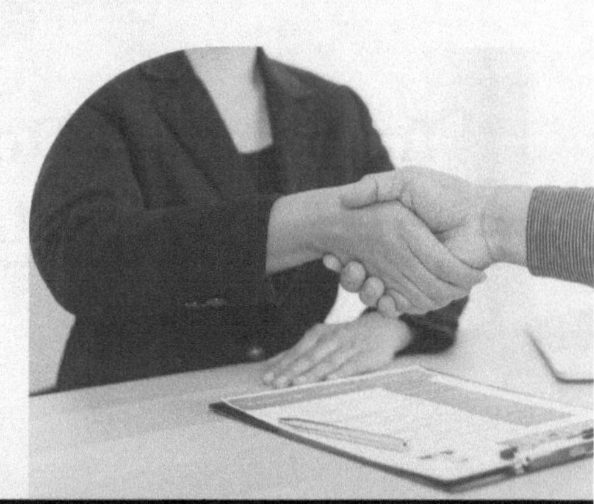

1. What is cryptography?
2. What distinguishes symmetric encryption from asymmetric encryption?
3. What is the CIA triad?
4. What are the different types of cyberattacks?
5. What is the difference between a vulnerability, a threat, and a risk?
6. What is your experience with security tools and technologies?

Chapter 14

Training and Documentation Department

Overview

TRAINING

JOIN US FOR A INSTRUCTOR-LED-TRAINING

WEDNESDAY, SEP 13, 2023, 7PM CST

LEARN HOW TO SELL:

- Discovery
- Cross/Upsell
- Renewal
- Much more!

WWW.LEADSYSTEMS.IN

Training is pivotal in the software industry as it enables individuals with the necessary skills and knowledge to excel in their respective roles. It provides a foundation for beginners and helps experienced professionals stay up-to-date with the latest trends and technologies. Through training, students can acquire technical and soft skills, such as programming languages, problem-solving, communication, and teamwork, which are highly valued in the industry.

Documentation is also crucial in ensuring compliance, quality assurance, and scalability. By documenting processes, standards, and guidelines, organizations can maintain consistency, reduce the risk of errors, and facilitate smooth collaboration among different departments. Furthermore, well-documented software systems enable easier maintenance, troubleshooting, and future enhancements, saving time and resources for the organization.

In conclusion, the importance of Training and Documentation in the software industry cannot be underestimated. Understanding and valuing the significance of these two aspects is essential for students aspiring to work in various software industry departments. Training enables employees with the skills and knowledge necessary to shine in their roles, while documentation ensures compliance and scalability. Embracing training and documentation is a key step toward becoming successful professionals in the dynamic and ever-growing software industry.

Key Functions of the Training and Documentation Team

The Training and Documentation team plays a vital role in any organization by providing employees with the knowledge and skills they need to be successful. The team's key functions include:

Creating and Maintaining Training Materials

This includes developing new training materials and updating existing materials to reflect changes in the product or process. The training materials should be clear, concise, engaging, and tailored to the learners' needs.

Delivering Training

This can be done in various ways, such as classroom training (ILT-Instructor-led training), online training (virtual), or on-the-job training (OJT). The training delivery method should be chosen based on the learners' needs and the training's content.

Supporting Learners

It includes answering questions, giving feedback, and helping learners troubleshoot problems. The training team should be available to learners throughout the training process to ensure success.

In addition to the above, the training and documentation team may also be involved in the following activities:

- Developing training plans involves creating a roadmap for delivering the necessary training to employees.
- Evaluating training effectiveness involves collecting data to determine whether it meets its objectives.
- Advising on training-related matters may involve advising managers and employees on training-related topics, such as the best way to deliver training or the most effective training methods.

The training and documentation team is a valuable asset to any organization. By effectively carrying out their duties, they can help the organization achieve its goals by ensuring its employees have the knowledge and skills they need to succeed.

Here are some of the benefits of having a well-functioning training and documentation team:

Increased Employee Productivity

Employees with the necessary knowledge and skills can significantly enhance organizational productivity. As a result, the organization stands to benefit from increased profits.

Reduced Errors

Properly trained employees are less likely to make errors. This can save the organization money in terms of wasted time and resources.

Improved Customer Service

Customer satisfaction improves when employees answer questions and resolve problems effectively.

Increased Compliance

When the organization has clear and up-to-date documentation, it is less likely to violate regulations. This can protect the companies from fines and penalties.

Enhanced Employee Morale

Employees who feel supported and have the needed knowledge and skills are more likely to be satisfied with their jobs. Promoting this fosters a more constructive work atmosphere, and the employee turnover rate can be diminished.

By taking these steps, you can ensure that your training and documentation team is effective in helping your organization achieve its goals.

Challenges and Strategies for Success

The Training and Documentation team is one of the key pillars for the success of any organization, whose primary role is to equip employees with the essential skills and knowledge required for efficient performance. However, several challenges may impede the progress and achievements of these teams.

Some of the most common challenges include:

Lack of Time and Resources

Training and Documentation can be time-consuming and expensive, and organizations often don't have the dedicated resources for these activities.

Employee Resistance to Change

Employees may resist change and be unmotivated to learn new skills or adopt new processes. This can make it challenging to get buy-in for training and documentation initiatives.

Lack of Coordination

Training and documentation can be a complex process, and it's important to have a well-coordinated approach. However, this cannot be easy to achieve, as different departments and teams may have different needs and priorities.

Despite these challenges, several strategies are used to improve the success of training and documentation teams. These include:

Conducting a Needs Assessment

The first step is to do TNA (Training need analysis) to identify the organization's training requirements. This will help to ensure that resources are used effectively.

Making it Engaging

Training and Documentation should be engaging and relevant to the audience's needs. This will help to keep them motivated and make it more likely that they will retain the information.

Providing Practice Opportunities

Employees need opportunities to practice what they have learned to master new skills. This can be done through On-the-Job Training (OJT), simulations, or other methods.

Evaluating the Results

It's important to evaluate the effectiveness of training and documentation initiatives to ensure they meet their goals. This information can be used to improve future efforts.

By addressing the challenges and implementing these strategies, training, and documentation teams can play a vital role in helping organizations achieve their goals.

Here are some additional tips for success based on personal experience.

- Get buy-in from senior management.
- Make training and documentation a priority.
- Tailor your approach to the needs of your audience.
- Use technology to your advantage.
- Measure your results and make improvements.

By following these tips, you can help your training and documentation team succeed in achieving its goals.

Important Aspects of the Training & Doc. Team

Training Needs Analysis and Curriculum Development

In the fast-paced and ever-evolving field of the software industry department, students must understand the importance of Training Needs Analysis (TNA) and Curriculum Development. Whether you aspire to work in Software Development, Quality Assurance, Project Management, User Experience Design, Technical Support, Sales and Marketing, Research and Development, Data Analytics, Cybersecurity, or Training and Documentation, this chapter will guide you in understanding the significance of these processes.

TNA is the systematic process of identifying the knowledge, skills, and competencies required by employees in a specific department or role. It involves assessing the current skill gaps and determining the training interventions to bridge them. By conducting a TNA, organizations can ensure their employees have the knowledge and abilities to perform their tasks effectively.

Curriculum development, on the other hand, focuses on designing and creating a structured program to address the identified training needs. This includes selecting appropriate learning materials, instructional methods, and evaluation strategies. A well-designed curriculum enhances employees' skills and aligns with the organization's goals and objectives.

A TNA can help identify the specific programming languages, development methodologies, and tools required for students interested in software development. Based on the TNA results, a curriculum can be developed to provide hands-on experience in coding, software architecture, and version control systems.

The importance of TNA and Curriculum Development extends to other departments, including Technical Support, Sales and Marketing, Research and Development, Data Analytics, Cybersecurity, and Training and Documentation.

In conclusion, TNA and Curriculum Development play a vital role in shaping the skills and competencies of students aspiring to work in various software industry departments. By understanding the needs and requirements of each department, students can acquire the necessary knowledge and skills to excel in their chosen field.

Instructional Design and Training Delivery Methods

Instructional design is the organic process of creating compelling and engaging learning experiences. It consists of analyzing the learner's needs, designing instructional materials, and assessing the effectiveness of the training program. Most Instructional designers use the ADDIE (Analyze, Design, Develop, Implement, and Evaluate) model to create training material to cater to the specific needs of their respective departments and customers.

Training delivery methods ensure employees acquire the necessary skills and knowledge to excel. Various delivery methods are available, and each has strengths and limitations. Some commonly used methods include Instructor-led Training (ILT), online courses, virtual classrooms, gamification, simulations, and hands-on workshops.

The choice of training delivery method depends on factors such as the complexity of the subject matter, the number of employees being trained, and the resources available. *For example, Instructor-led training is ideal for complex topics that require direct interaction with an expert, while online courses may be more suitable for self-paced learning.*

Regardless of the chosen delivery method, it is essential to consider adult learning principles. Adults learn best when actively engaged when the training is relevant to their job roles, and when they can apply the concepts in real-world scenarios. Incorporating interactive elements like quizzes, case studies, and group discussions can enhance the learning experience and improve knowledge retention.

Furthermore, technology plays a significant role in modern Instructional design. Learning Management Systems (LMS) enable organizations to deliver, track, and manage training programs effectively. Interactive multimedia, such as videos, gamification, and simulations, can also enhance the learning experience and make it more engaging.

In conclusion, instructional design and training delivery methods are integral to the company's success.

Technical Writing and Documentation Standards

Technical writing involves the creation of clear, concise, and accurate documentation for various purposes. It serves as a guide for users, a reference for developers, and a means of communication between different organizational departments. Adhering to technical writing and documentation standards ensures your work is easily understood, consistent, and accessible to everyone involved.

One of the important aspects of technical writing is maintaining a standardized format. This includes using consistent terminology, headings, fonts, and layouts throughout your documentation. Having a standardized format improves the readability of your content and presents a unified and professional image for your department.

Using plain language and avoiding jargon, acronyms, and technical terms that might confuse your readers is crucial. Instead, opt for clear and straightforward explanations in everyday language. Use examples, diagrams, and step-by-step instructions to make complex concepts more accessible.

Additionally, it is crucial to keep your documentation up to date. As software evolves, new features are added, and bugs are fixed. Ensure that your documentation reflects these changes accurately and promptly. Constant review and updating of content helps maintain its relevance and usefulness.

In technical writing and documentation, collaboration plays a vital role. Engage subject matter experts from different departments to guarantee the accuracy and comprehensiveness of your content. Seek feedback from users and stakeholders to improve your documentation's quality continuously.

Lastly, consider the different needs and preferences of your audience. Some prefer printed manuals, while others prefer online documentation or video tutorials. Provide multiple formats and delivery methods to cater to diverse users.

In conclusion, Technical Writing and Documentation standards are essential for effective communication within the software industry department. By adhering to a standardized format, using plain language, keeping content up to date, collaborating with experts, and considering audience preferences, you can create high-quality documentation that enhances productivity, knowledge sharing, and overall success within your department.

Training and Documentation Dept Hierarchy – Generalized View

In the software industry, the training team certifies that employees have the necessary skills and knowledge to excel. The job hierarchy within the training team can vary from one organization to another, but here is a generalized structure that you might find in many software companies.

Director Training or Enablement

The Director is at the top of the hierarchy. The owner defines the entire training function within the organization. They develop the training strategy, set goals, and manage the budget for training initiatives. They also collaborate with other departments to align training programs with business objectives.

Training Manager

Reporting to the Director, the Training Manager supervises the daily operations of the training team. They assist in planning and implementing training programs, manage a team of trainers, and ensure that training materials are up-to-date.

Trainers/Instructional Designers

Trainers are responsible for enabling employees. They have in-depth knowledge of the software products, processes, and technologies used in the company. Instructional Designers work closely with trainers to develop training materials, including e-learning, courses, and documentation.

Subject Matter Experts (SMEs)

SMEs are experts in specific areas of software development, such as programming languages, frameworks, or tools. They collaborate with trainers and instructional designers to ensure that training content is accurate and latest.

Training Coordinators/Administrators

Training Coordinators or Administrators provide logistical support for training programs. They schedule training sessions, manage enrollments, and handle administrative tasks related to training initiatives. Training may range from new hire onboarding programs to employees seeking skill development.

Content Developers

Content Developers are responsible for creating and updating training materials. They work closely with instructional designers to produce e-learning modules, videos, documentation, and other resources.

LMS Administrators

LMS Administrators manage the technical aspects of the LMS platform. They ensure that courses are uploaded and accessible and track learner progress.

This hierarchy can be more extensive in larger organizations, with specialized roles and additional layers. However, some of these roles may be combined or have fewer formal distinctions in smaller software companies.

Training and Documentation Interview Questions

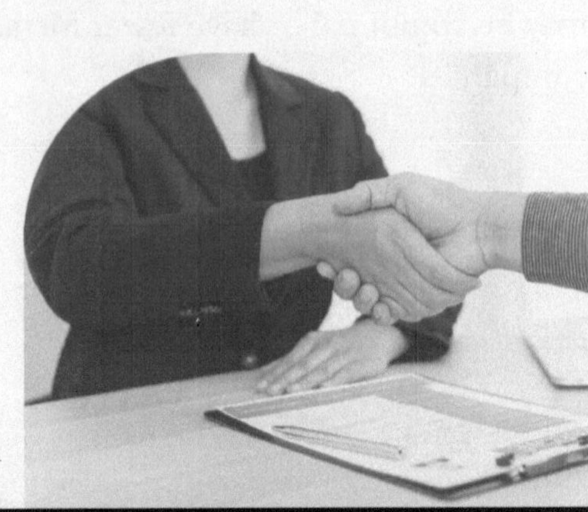

1. What is your experience developing and delivering software product training programs?
2. How do you stay up-to-date on the latest software trends and technologies?
3. What is your experience with creating and maintaining content?
4. How do you use technology to enhance the training and documentation experience?
5. How do you measure the effectiveness of your training and content delivered?

Chapter 15

Conceptualizing Using Real-World Scenario

Case Study: A Home Renovation Project

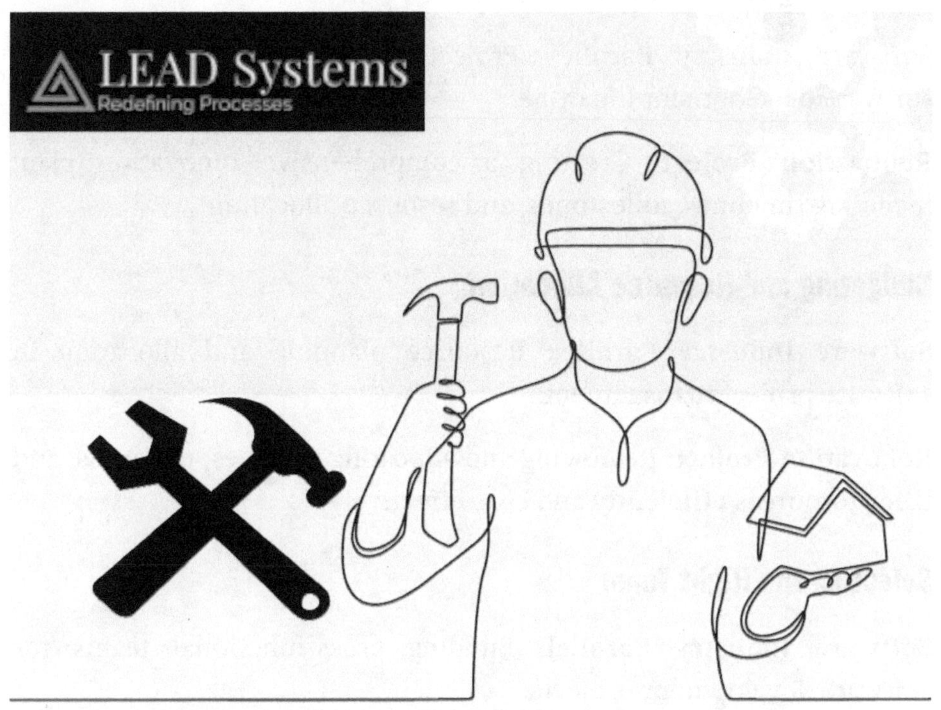

HOME RENOVATION PROJECT

Abstract: This case study delves into the details of planning and executing a home renovation project, drawing parallels to the software industry. The study emphasizes the importance of strategic thinking, project management, and process-oriented approaches in both domains.

Defining Requirements

Software Industry Parallel: Requirement gathering and analysis phase in software development.

Renovation Project: Detailed assessment of the existing structure, identifying functional and aesthetic needs, and setting project goals.

Establishing Roadmap

Software Industry Parallel: Project planning and scheduling in software development life cycle.

Renovation Project: Creating a comprehensive renovation plan, including timelines, milestones, and resource allocation.

Budgeting and Resource Allocation

Software Industry Parallel: Resource planning and allocation in software project management.

Renovation Project: Reviewing and allocating finances, materials, and labor resources efficiently and cost-effectively.

Selecting the Right Team

Software Industry Parallel: Building cross-functional teams for software development projects.

Renovation Project: Choosing skilled professionals (Architects) and coordinating their efforts to ensure a cohesive project execution.

Agile Adaptation

Software Industry Parallel: Agile methodology for iterative software development.

Renovation Project: Embracing adaptability and making real-time adjustments to the renovation plan based on evolving requirements.

Quality Assurance

Software Industry Parallel: Testing and quality assurance in software development.

Renovation Project: Implementing rigorous quality checks at various stages to ensure the construction material meets desired standards.

Communication and Collaboration

Software Industry Parallel: Effective communication within development teams.

Renovation Project: Establishing clear communication channels between the client, contractor, and the renovation team.

Risk Management

Software Industry Parallel: Identifying and mitigating risks in software projects. **Renovation Project**: Proactively assessing potential risks in the renovation process and implementing contingency plans for delays.

Monitoring and Progress Tracking

Software Industry Parallel: Project monitoring and progress tracking in software development.

Renovation Project: Using key performance indicators (KPIs) to track the progress of the renovation project against established milestones.

Documentation and Knowledge Transfer

Software Industry Parallel: Documentation and knowledge sharing in software development.

Renovation Project: Maintaining detailed records of the renovation process for future reference and potential resale.

Analysing and Summarising Scenario

Read the scenario below and see how closely you can relate the Software Industry Departments with the Real-World example.

Planning

The first step in planning a home renovation project is to define your goals. What do you want to achieve with your renovation? Are you looking to improve the functionality of your space, increase its value, or create a more stylish and comfortable home? Once you understand your goals well, you can develop a plan. When developing your plan, it is vital to consider the following factors:

Budget

How much money are you willing to spend on your renovation? It is essential to be realistic about your budget and factor in all potential costs, including materials, labor, and permits.

Timeline

How long do you want your renovation to take? Remember that renovations can often take longer than expected, so it is essential to set realistic expectations.

Scope of work

What tasks you must complete to achieve your goals? Once you understand the scope of work, you can develop a schedule and identify the necessary resources.

Execution

Once you have a plan, it is time to start executing your renovation project. Here are some tips for a successful execution:

Communicate with your team

Communicate your expectations clearly to your contractors. It is also essential to keep them updated on your progress and to be responsive to their questions and concerns.

Be Flexible

Things don't always go as planned during a renovation project. Be prepared to make adjustments as needed.

Be Patient

Home renovations can be stressful, but it is essential to be patient and enjoy the process. Remember that the result will be a home that you love.

Conclusion

Recapitulation of the successful execution of the home renovation project through the application of software industry principles. Emphasis on the significance of strategic thinking, process-oriented approaches, and effective project management in achieving desired outcomes.

Assignment for you

Create a case study parallels between "Organizing and managing a family vacation" and the operations of various departments within the software industry based on the above example for another real-world example.

For validation, you may share it on my email id: **sanjay@leadsystems.in**

Chapter 16

Jargon, Tools and Certifications

A Quick Review

Numerous career opportunities and paths are available in the software industry for students interested in pursuing a career in this constantly changing field. This section introduces different departments' keywords or jargon, widely used tools within the software industry, and the certifications offered in these trades.

Human Resource Department

This Department plays a crucial role in managing and nurturing the workforce, ensuring the right talent is in place to drive innovation and growth.

#Keywords: Recruiting, Talent, Onboarding, Workforce, Retention, Conflict, Relationship

#Tools: Human Resource Information System (HRIS), Application tracking system (ATS), Learning Management System (LMS), Zoom, Slack, Bluejeans.

#Certifications: SHRM Certified Professional (SHRM-CP), Professional in Human Resources (PHR), Certified Human Resources Professional (CHRP), Talent Management Practitioner.

Finance and Administration

This Department is responsible for creating the process of planning, organizing, directing, and controlling an organization's financial resources. Financial management is essential in the software industry due to the high cost of developing and marketing software products.

#Keywords: Budgeting, Forecasting, Operational cost, Cost center, Planning, Balance sheet, Cash flow, Backup, Restoring, Security awareness, IT Infra.

#Tools: Accounting software like Quickbooks, Xero, Sage Intacct. Expense tracking software like Zoho Concur. Budgeting software like

Mint and Personal Capital. Payroll software like ADP and Gusto. Tax prep tools like TurboTax TaxAct.

#Certifications: Chartered Financial Analyst (CFA), Certified Public Accountant (CPA), Certified Financial Planner (CFP), Certified Management Accountant (CMA), Certified Administrative Professional (CAP).

Legal and Compliance

This Department is responsible for the processes and procedures the company puts in place to ensure it complies with laws and regulations related to privacy, security, intellectual property, and employment.

#Keywords: Privacy, Security, GDPR, Laws, Access, Control, Encryption

#Tools: Compliance management software, Data privacy software, Auditing software

#Certifications: Certified Compliance and Ethics Professional (CCEP), Certified Regulatory Compliance Manager (CRCM), Certified Information Systems Auditor (CISA), Certified Fraud Examiner (CFE)

Software Development Department

This Department is responsible for designing, coding, and testing software applications. Software development careers include engineers, front-end developers, back-end developers, full-stack developers, UX designers, interaction designers, information architects, and mobile app developers.

#Keywords: Agile, Scrum, Kanban, DevOps, Full-Stack, Cloud, AI, ML, UI, Open source, Web and Mobile development, Data Science, and Code review.

#Tools: Version control systems like Git and GitHub, Integrated development environments (IDEs) like Visual Studio and Eclipse, Debuggers like GDB and Visual Studio Debugger, DevOps tools like

Ansible and Puppet, Design tools like Figma and Sketch, Documentation tools like Confluence and Doxygen, Communication tools like Slack and Zoom, Code editors like Sublime Text and Atom, Build tools like Maven and Gradle, Cloud computing platforms like AWS, Azure, and Google Cloud Platform

#Certifications: AWS Certified Developer, Google Professional Cloud Developer, Microsoft Certified Azure Developer, OCP, Certified Scrum developer, AWS DevOps Engineer.

Quality Assurance Department

The Quality Assurance Department ensures software products meet high quality and functionality standards. Career paths in this department include software tester, quality assurance engineer, and test automation engineer.

#Keywords: Standards, Review, User experience, Testing, Feedback, Validation, Auditing, Performance metrics and Reporting.

#Tools: Test management tools like TestRail, Jira, and Zephyr. Functional testing tools like Selenium, Katalon Studio, and SoapUI. Performance testing tools like JMeter, LoadRunner, and NeoLoad. Security testing tools like OWASP ZAP, Burp Suite, and Nessus. Usability testing tools like UserZoom, Maze, and Validately. Automated testing tools like Testsigma, Appium, and Ranorex.

#Certifications: ISTQB Certified Tester, Certified Quality Engineer (CQE) by American Society for Quality (ASQ), International Six Sigma Black Belt, Compliance,

Project Management Department

The Project Management Department oversees the successful completion of software projects. Project management care includes project managers, scrum masters, and product owners.

#Keywords: Planning, Execution, Risk, Management, Team, PMO, PMLC, Communication, Closure, Budget and Time.

#Tools: Project management tools like Jira, Wrike, Asana, Trello, and Monday.com

#Certifications: PMP, Prince2, CAPM, ACP, CSM and ITIL

Technical Support Department

The Technical Support Department assists and resolves technical issues for software users. Technical support workers include specialists, help desk technicians, and customer support representatives.

#Keywords: Customer, Issue, Knowledge Article, SLA, RCA, Troubleshooting, Case, Bug.

#Tools: Ticketing system, Knowledge base, Remote access software, Live chat, Customer feedback surveys.

#Certifications: CompTIA A+, Google IT Support Professional Certificate, CCNA, Salesforce Certifications.

Sales and Marketing Department

This Department promotes and sells software products to potential customers. Careers in Sales and Marketing include sales representatives, account managers, and product marketing managers.

#Keywords: Quota, Campaign, Incentive, Rewards, Reporting, Account, Leads, Opportunity, Nurture, Deal, Revenue, Prospect.

#Tools: Customer relationship management (CRM) software like Salesforce, HubSpot, and Zoho. Sales intelligence tools like ZoomInfo, Sales Navigator, and LeadIQ. Sales acceleration like Outreach, SalesLoft. Data connectors and integration tools like Zapier, Integromat, and Microsoft Power Automate. Sales analytics like Salesforce Einstein Analytics, HubSpot, and Zoho SalesIQ.

#Certifications: CSP, PCM (Digital Marketing), Certified Advertising Specialist (CAS), Certified Management Accountant (CMA), Accredited Business Communicator (ABC)

Research and Development Department

The Research and Development Department explores new technologies and innovative software solutions. Careers in research and development include research scientists, software architects, and innovation engineers.

#Keywords: Scientist, Innovation, Idea, Problem-Solving, Critical Thinking, Engineering.

#Tools: Technology scouting tools like IGOR^AI, Wellspring, and Ezassi. Software-powered services like Findest, Luxresearch, and Yet2. Science search engines like Web of Science, Microsoft Academic, and Google Scholar. Intellectual property tools like Google Patents, Patsnap, and Patent Inspiration. Startup scouting tools like dealroom. co, crunchbase, and FUELUP. Idea management tools like SkipsoLabs, IDEA DROP, and ideanote.io. New product development tools like Jama software, Planview, and Elemental machines. Market intelligence/ trends like Gartner and CB Insights.

#Certifications: Certificated Innovation Professional (CIP), Salesforce Certified Solution Architect, Open CA, AWS Certified Solutions Architect, Microsoft Certified Solutions Expert (MCSE), Certified Information Systems Security Professional - Architecture (CISSP-ISSAP)

Data Analytics Department

The Data Analytics Department analyzes and interprets data to derive meaningful insights for the business. Careers in data analytics include data analysts, data scientists, and business intelligence analysts.

#Keywords: Data visualization, Data mining, Machine learning, Big data, SQL, Tableau, Python, Power BI, Accuracy, intelligence.

#Tools: Data Analytics tools like Microsoft Power BI, Tableau, Qlik Sense, Looker, Zoho Analytics, Domo, SAS Viya, R, and Python.

#Certifications: Google Data Analytics Professional Certificate, IBM Data Analyst Professional Certificate, Microsoft Certified: Power BI Data Analyst Associate, AWS Certified Data Analytics, SAS Certified Data Scientist

Cybersecurity Department

The Cybersecurity Department ensures the security of software systems and protects against cyber threats. Careers in cybersecurity include cybersecurity analysts, ethical hackers, and security engineers.

#Keywords: Threat, Risk, Virus, Malware, Firewall, Authentication, Authorization, Encryption, Phishing, Ransomware, Vulnerabilities.

#Tools: CyberSecurity tools like Nikto, SQLMap, KisMac, WireSharkBurp Suite, and NetStumbler.

#Certifications: Certified Information Systems Security Professional (CISSP), Certified Ethical Hacker (CEH), Certified Information Systems Auditor (CISA), Certified Information Security Manager (CISM),

Training and Documentation Department

The Training and Documentation Department creates user manuals and provides training materials for software products. The training and documentation team includes technical writers, instructional designers, trainers, training program managers, and technical trainers.

#Keywords: Enablement, Roadmap, Nesting, Onboarding, Training Calendar, Content, Schedule, ADDIE, TNA, Standards, Guidelines, Curriculum, Tutorials, Gamification, Compliance.

#Tools: Training and Documentation tools like Document360, Bit.ai, Proprofs, Confluence and Jira.

#Certifications: Certified Professional in Training and Development (CPTD), Certified Technical Professional (CTP), Certified Professional in Learning and Performance (CPLP), Certified Content Developer (CCD), Certified Instructional Designer (CID), Certified Training Specialist (CTS)

Students must explore their interests and skills to determine which department best aligns with their career goals. Moreover, the software industry encourages interdisciplinary collaboration, allowing professionals to transition between departments and explore various career paths within the same company. It is called IJP (Internal Job Posting) in the corporate world. Continuous learning and following up with industry trends are crucial for success in the software industry.

In conclusion, the software industry offers various career opportunities and paths across multiple departments. Whether your passion lies in Software Development, Quality Assurance, Project Management, User Experience Design, Technical Support, Sales and Marketing, Research and Development, Data Analytics, Cybersecurity, or Training and Documentation, there is a place for you in the software industry. Embrace the opportunities, continue learning, and be prepared for a rewarding and fulfilling career in the dynamic world of software.

Tips for Success in the Software Industry

The Software Industry is a dynamic and fast-paced field that offers excellent career opportunities for students. Whether you aspire to work in any of the departments mentioned above, the following tips will help you succeed.

Continuous Learning

As the saying goes, change is inevitable, which also holds for the software industry. You can effectively enhance your skills and knowledge by enrolling in courses, attending workshops and conferences, and actively participating in online forums. This proactive approach will help you to stay abreast of the latest technologies and tools.

Networking

Build a solid professional network within the software industry. Attend industry events, join online communities, and connect with professionals on platforms like LinkedIn. Networking can open doors to job opportunities, mentorship, and valuable advice.

Internships and Projects

Gain practical experience by undertaking internships or working on software projects during your studies. This hands-on experience will not only enhance your technical skills but also provide you with real-world insights into the software industry.

Collaboration

The Software Industry thrives on collaboration. Work effectively in teams, communicate clearly, and be open to feedback. Collaborating with colleagues from different departments will broaden your knowledge and help you develop a well-rounded skill set.

Problem-Solving Skills

Develop strong problem-solving abilities, which are highly valued in the software industry. Practice logical thinking, break down complex problems into manageable tasks, and adopt a solution-oriented approach.

Attention to Detail

Software Development requires a keen eye for detail. Pay attention to coding standards, debugging, and testing. Even the most minor lapse can lead to critical issues later, so be meticulous.

Adaptability

The Software Industry is known for its rapid changes and evolving technologies. Be adaptable and embrace new tools, languages, and frameworks. Stay flexible and open-minded to stay ahead of the curve.

Communication Skills

Effective communication is essential in every department of the software industry. It is important to cultivate proficient written and verbal communication abilities to express ideas, collaborate effectively with team members, and successfully communicate technical concepts to individuals who may not have a technical background.

Time Management

Deadlines are a part of the software industry. Learn to prioritize tasks, manage time efficiently, and deliver quality work within time constraints.

Professionalism

Maintain a professional attitude in all aspects of your work. Be punctual, respectful, and ethical. Demonstrate accountability and integrity in your actions.

By following these tips, you will be well-equipped to succeed in the software industry. Continuous learning, adaptability, collaboration, and problem-solving skills are vital to thriving in this ever-evolving field. Good luck in your software industry career!

Glossary

Definitions of Key Terms and Concepts

Understanding the language and terminology used in the software industry is essential for students aiming to excel in various software industry departments. This aims to provide an overview of key terms and concepts commonly used in software development, quality assurance, project management, user experience (UX) design, technical support, sales and marketing, research and development, data analytics, cybersecurity, training, and documentation.

Agile: *Agile is a set of principles that emphasize flexibility, collaboration, and continuous improvement*

Scrum: *Scrum is a framework for agile implementation that assists teams in organizing and overseeing their work by employing a collection of values, principles, and practices.*

Kanban: *Kanban is a workflow management methodology that helps teams visualize work, limit work in progress, and optimize flow.*

DevOps: *DevOps combines software development and IT operations to streamline the systems development life cycle and ensure continuous delivery of high-quality software.*

Full-Stack: *Full-stack developer is a person who can work on both the front end and the back end of a web application.*

Cloud: *The term "cloud" is often used as a metaphor for the Internet, but it can also refer to a specific type of computing environment.*

AI *is a computer science stream that concentrates on developing intelligent systems capable of carrying out tasks that usually necessitate human intelligence.*

UI: *UI stands for user interface. It is the part of a product that allows users to interact with it.*

Web Development: *Web development encompasses designing and coding websites using languages like HTML, CSS, JavaScript, and PHP.*

Mobile development: *Mobile development is the process of creating mobile apps. This includes native apps, built specifically for a particular platform (such as iOS or Android), and hybrid apps, built using web technologies but can be installed on a mobile device. Mobile developers use a variety of languages and tools, including Java, Kotlin, Swift, Objective-C, and React Native.*

Data Science *Data science uses scientific methods to extract knowledge and insights from data.*

Code Review: *Code review involves the evaluation of a program's source code to ensure its quality and functionality.*

Standards: *A standard is a set of rules, guidelines, or specifications that are used to measure the quality, performance, or consistency of something.*

Review: *A review is a process of inspecting and evaluating a product or service to ensure that it meets its requirements and expectations*

User experience: *User experience (UX) refers to how users experience a product, system, or service.*

Testing: *Software testing ensures a software product or application performs as intended.*

Feedback: *Feedback is information about the quality of a product or service that is provided to the people responsible for creating or delivering it*

Validation: Validation establishes documented evidence that a process consistently produces a product meeting predetermined specifications and quality attributes.

Auditing: *Auditing is the process of inspecting and evaluating a software product, process, or system to ensure that it meets predetermined standards*

Performance metrics: *Performance metrics are quantitative measurements that assess software performance, quality, and team productivity.*

Reporting: *Reporting involves collecting and analyzing data to present it as user-friendly.*

Planning: *Planning is the process of defining the project scope, deliverables, timeline, budget, and resources needed to complete the project*

Execution: *Execution is the phase in which the project plan is put into action, and the actual work is performed*

Risk: *An uncertain event or condition occurs that may have a positive or negative effect on a project's objectives*

Risk Management: *The process of identifying, analyzing, and responding to any risk that could impact the project's objectives*

PMO: *A Project Management Office (PMO) establishes and maintains project management standards within an organization.*

PMLC: *It stands for Project Management Life Cycle. It is a framework that breaks down a project into a series of phases, each with its goals and deliverables.*

Communication: *The process of exchanging information and ideas between project stakeholders.*

Stakeholders *are any individual, group, or organization interested in a project's outcome.*

Closure: *The process of formally ending a project. It involves completing all outstanding tasks, collecting and archiving project documentation, and obtaining sign-off from all stakeholders.*

Budget: *A budget estimates the total cost of a project over a specific period.*

Time management: *Planning, scheduling, monitoring, and controlling the time spent on project tasks and activities.*

Customer: *A customer is anyone who has purchased or uses a company's products or services.*

Issue: *A customer has a problem with a product or service.*

Knowledge Article: *It is documentation that answers a frequently asked question or provides instructions for solving a problem that customers commonly run into*

SLA: *An SLA (service-level agreement) is a contract between the department and its customers that defines the level of service that will be provided*

RCA: *It stands for Root Cause Analysis. It is a systematic process for identifying the underlying cause of a problem.*

Troubleshooting: *the process of identifying and resolving problems in a technical system. Technical support professionals need the skill of quickly identifying and resolving issues.*

Case: *A case records an interaction between a customer and a technical support representative.*

Bug: *An unexpected issue with software or hardware hinders its intended use.*

Quota: *A quota is a numerical goal that sales representatives or teams are expected to achieve in a given period. Quotas can be set based on revenue, closed deals, or other relevant metrics.*

Campaign: *A campaign involves coordinated marketing and sales activities to achieve specific goals.*

Incentive: *An incentive rewards salespeople or marketers for achieving specific goals.*

QBR: *QBR stands for Quarterly Business Review. It is a meeting between sales reps, managers, and other stakeholders to discuss the previous quarter's performance and plan for the upcoming quarter.*

Accounts: *It refers to the specific customers or clients*

Leads: *A potential customer who has shown interest in your product or service*

Opportunity: *An opportunity is a qualified lead likely to become a paying customer.*

Nurture: *After converting a LEAD (Prospect) into an Account (Company), building relationships with potential customers, and providing their services for a long-term relationship.*

Deal: *It is a potential sale that has been identified and qualified*

Revenue: *Revenue is a company's money from selling its software products or services.*

Innovation: *Introducing new ideas, methods, or technologies that bring about positive changes in software development practices, products, or services.*

Prototyping: *Creating an initial version of a software product to demonstrate its functionality and design, helping stakeholders visualize the final product and gather feedback.*

Proof of Concept (PoC): *A small-scale demonstration or prototype to validate the feasibility and potential of a software idea or technology before committing to full-scale development.*

Algorithm Optimization: *Refining and enhancing the efficiency of algorithms used in software applications to ensure faster processing, reduced resource consumption, and improved performance.*

Machine Learning: *ML enables software to learn from historical data, make predictions, and improve performance over time. It is a subset of AI.*

Open Source: *Application whose source code is public, allowing collaboration, modification, and redistribution by anyone, fostering innovation and community-driven development.*

Version Control: *Managing changes to software code over time, enabling collaboration among developers, tracking modifications, and ensuring a coherent development history.*

Cybersecurity: *The practice of protecting software applications and systems from cyber threats, including unauthorized access, data breaches, and other malicious activities.*

API (Application Programming Interface): *A set of protocols and tools that allows different software components to communicate and interact, enabling integration between diverse systems.*

Cloud Computing: *The way to access computing resources, such as servers, storage, and applications, over the internet. This means that you don't need to own or manage your hardware and software, which can save you money and time.*

User Experience (UX) Design: *Creating software interfaces that are intuitive, user-friendly, and aligned with the needs and preferences of the end-users.*

Data analytics: *Converting raw data into meaningful information used to make better decisions.*

Data mining: *The process of extracting knowledge from large datasets.*

Business intelligence: *A broad term that encompasses the applications, technologies, and processes used to collect, analyze, and present business data.*

Data visualization: *Graphical representations of data to communicate information more effectively.*

Data Governance: *Establishing policies, processes, and controls to ensure the quality, security, and proper usage of data throughout an organization.*

Dashboard: *Executive summary showcasing key metrics and performance indicators in visual representation depicting a real-time overview of an organization's performance.*

ETL (Extract, Transform, Load): *The procedure of collecting data from diverse sources, standardizing it into a uniform format, and storing it in a data repository for analysis.*

Business Intelligence (BI): *Technologies, applications, and practices for collecting, integrating, analyzing, and presenting business information to enable informed decision-making.*

Big Data: *The term "big data" pertains to the enormous amount of structured and unstructured information organizations produce daily. Given its vast quantity and intricate nature, it necessitates specific tools and methods for examination.*

Predictive Analytics: *By utilizing historical data, statistical algorithms, and ML techniques, it becomes possible to determine the probability of future outcomes or trends.*

Descriptive Analytics: *The analysis of past data to understand what has happened and gain insights into historical trends and patterns.*

SQL: *A programming language used for managing data in relational databases. SQL is a critical skill for data analysts, allowing them to extract data from databases and perform complex queries.*

Data modeling: *Creating a conceptual data model to represent real-world entities and their relationships.*

Tableau: *Tableau is a platform that helps people explore, analyze, and share data.*

Python: *Python is a popular programming language (open-source) used in the data analytics department in the software industry.*

Power BI: *A business intelligence (BI) tool used to collect, analyze, and visualize data.*

Cybersecurity: *Protecting systems, networks, and data from unauthorized access, use, disclosure, disruption, modification, or destruction.*

Information security: *The protection of information from unauthorized access, use, disclosure, disruption, modification, or destruction.*

ISO 27001: *An international standard that provides best practices for information security management.*

Ethical hacking: *Hacking into a system or network with permission to identify and fix security vulnerabilities.*

Network security: *The practice of protecting computer networks from unauthorized access, use, disclosure, vulnerability, modification, or destruction.*

Security information and event management (SIEM): *It records and analyzes security logs and events from multiple sources to identify potential threats.*

Vulnerability management: *Identifying, assessing, and mitigating security vulnerabilities in systems and networks.*

Incident response: *Responding to and recovering from a cybersecurity incident.*

Cloud security: *Protecting data and applications available on a cloud from unauthorized access, use, exposure, modification, or deletion.*

Phishing: *It refers to a malicious activity where cybercriminals attempt to deceive individuals into divulging sensitive information, such as passwords, credit card details, or personal data, by posing as a legitimate entity.*

Onboarding: *Introducing new employees to a company and its culture. Onboarding training typically covers company policies, procedures, and products or services.*

Technical training *teaches employees the skills they need to perform their jobs. Specialized training can cover programming languages, software development methodologies, and cloud computing.*

Soft skills training: *Training that teaches employees the non-technical skills they need to be successful in the workplace. Soft skills training can cover communication, teamwork, and problem-solving topics.*

Continuing education: *Training that helps employees stay up to date on the modern trends and technologies in their field. Continuing education can be provided in-house, through online courses, or at conferences and workshops.*

E-learning: *An online training method through a learning management system (LMS). E-learning can be asynchronous (self-paced) or synchronous (live).*

Blended learning: *A blend of e-learning and traditional classroom training. This can be a cost-effective way to deliver training.*

Assessment: *Measuring employees' knowledge, skills, and abilities. Review helps to access the knowledge gap, track progress, and measure the training program's effectiveness.*

Evaluation: *The process of determining the value of a training program. Evaluation helps to assess the impact of training on employee performance, satisfaction, and retention.*

TNA: *TNA stands for "Training Needs Analysis." It is a process to identify individuals' knowledge gaps, skills, and abilities within an organization or a specific context.*

Roadmap: *A roadmap is a strategic plan that outlines the goals, objectives, and critical steps required to achieve a particular outcome or vision.*

Compliance: *It refers to adherence to regulatory and industry standards, policies, and guidelines within information technology education.*

www.ingramcontent.com/pod-product-compliance
Lightning Source LLC
LaVergne TN
LVHW091315150826
845673LV00006B/1648

* 9 7 9 8 8 9 1 3 3 8 9 1 3 *